Getting Started in
MODEL
RAILROADING

Jeff Wilson

KB
KALMBACH BOOKS
WAUKESHA, WI

Kalmbach Books
21027 Crossroads Circle
Waukesha, Wisconsin 53186
www.Kalmbach.com/Books

Published in 2016
20 19 18 17 16   1 2 3 4 5

Manufactured in China

ISBN: 978-1-62700-267-7
EISBN: 978-1-62700-268-4

Editor: Randy Rehberg
Book Design: Tom Ford

Unless noted, photographs were taken by the author.

Library of Congress Control Number: 2016931471

Contents

CHAPTER ONE

Basics of model railroading

John Callahan's HO scale model railroad turns the clock back to mid-1950s New England. His East Berkshire Branch, based on the prototype (actual) Rutland and Boston & Maine railroads, takes up a 14 x 21-foot area in the basement of his home. Detailed scenery, track on multiple levels, and weathering all make this scene realistic. *Lou Sassi*

Scale model railroading has been a compelling hobby since the early 1900s. The fascination of miniatures and the ability to build and create models, combined with the animation of trains that actually move along the track, has long been an attraction for people—even those who aren't actually hobbyists.

Steve Montgomery's HO Carol Valley Railroad epitomizes a modern model railroad (although set in the 1950s). The 13 x 18-foot layout uses Digital Command Control with walkaround operation enabled by handheld throttles. *Lou Sassi*

Much of model railroading's appeal is that it has so many facets. Although a common goal among model railroaders is the building of a complete scenicked, operating layout, most modelers gravitate toward specific areas of the hobby that interest them. This can mean building structures, detailing locomotives and rolling stock, creating scenery, or operating trains in a realistic manner. Many have or develop a strong interest in prototype (real) railroad history, including specific railroads, industries served by rail, or types of railroads such as logging or mountain lines. For many, this interest becomes a hobby unto itself, along with being a guide to modeling.

Another great appeal of the hobby is the ability to re-create a bygone time by modeling a specific era. You can create a miniature time machine that takes you back to the days of steam locomotives, highlights an interest in classic vehicles and old structures, or represents scenes and equipment that no longer exist in real life.

No single book can show you everything you need to know about the hobby. Instead, I'll highlight various areas of model railroading and model building, look at the hobby's history, examine various modeling scales, direct you to more detailed sources of information, and look at the pros and cons of various modeling techniques and materials.

Let's start with a look at how the hobby of scale modeling evolved from toy trains.

Toy trains vs. scale models

Toys depicting trains have been around since the mid-1800s. Most early toys were wooden carvings, followed by stamped-metal and cast-metal toys from the late 1800s into the early 1900s.

Early toy trains, into the 1900s, were simply meant to be pushed or pulled, or had windup clockwork mechanisms. By 1900, advances in technology led to electric trains that were powered by batteries or hand-cranked dynamos.

Toy trains quickly became a favorite for children, especially at Christmas. Manufacturers such as Ives, Lionel, Marx, and American Flyer offered complete train sets as well as individual locomotives, cars, track components, and many other accessories. As electrification spread from cities to rural areas, trains powered by plug-in transformers became commonplace.

The trains themselves became more realistic, with brightly lithographed tin bodies representing—if not exactly matching—real paint schemes and, in some cases, specific locomotives. The tin material gave these toys their "tinplate" moniker, a term that is often still used to describe toy trains to differentiate them from scale models.

The growing toy train market spawned a new hobby, as individuals—mainly adults—became interested in taking the toy trains and modifying them to be more realistic. By modifying models, laying track on tables and other permanent fixtures, and adding scenery and buildings, these early modelers created the first permanent model railroads.

By the 1930s, there were enough scale train enthusiasts to spawn the first magazine dedicated exclusively to the hobby: *The Model Railroader*, which

Bill Darnaby's HO scale Maumee Route is a fine example of a freelanced model railroad. Bill based his layout's features, name, and paint scheme on the Nickel Plate Road and other Midwestern prototype railroads. *Bill Darnaby*

was launched in 1934. Other early magazines, including *The Model Maker* and *The Model Craftsman* (which became *Railroad Model Craftsman* in 1949), highlighted scale railroad models along with ships, cars, and other types of scale models.

The scale side of the hobby grew dramatically from the 1940s onward, with an increase in the number of manufacturers devoted to producing models and kits built to scale. Com-

panies such as Varney, Globe, Bowser, Tru-Scale, and Walthers led the way with locomotive and rolling stock models and kits, detail parts, and structure kits.

Materials have evolved since those early days, from die-cast metal, wood, and early Bakelite plastic to injection-molded styrene, resin, and laser-cut wood. Manufacturing processes and printing and painting capabilities have also improved, which has led to a dramatic increase in the quality of models.

Toy trains are still made, and many are technologically quite advanced, but collecting and operating them remains a distinctive subset of the hobby. This book concentrates on the hobby of

scale model railroading, with the focus on creating accurate models and layouts that try to be as realistic as possible.

Basic hobby terms

As you get into the hobby, you'll be confronted by many terms and phrases, some of which are self-explanatory, but others that might leave you puzzled or might not mean exactly what they sound like. The rest of this book will explain many of these in detail, but here's a brief list.

In the hobby, the word *prototype* refers to real-life (full-size) railroading, helping distinguish full-size equipment from models. For example, you may read, "The HO scale model boxcar from Kadee is based on the prototype

The June 1939 issue of *The Model Railroader* included ads for companies producing scale kits and ready-to-run models in O and HO scales.

Common modeling scales include, from front: Z, N, HO, S, and O. All are models of 40-foot cars, from the 2¾₁₆"-long Z scale refrigerator car to the 10" O scale stock car.

Railroading timeline

Railroading has a long, complicated, fascinating history. It can be difficult for beginners to sort out information such as when certain railroads existed or when steam locomotives ceased operations. This listing is far from complete, but it provides a rough idea of how railroads evolved from 1900 through today.

1900: Small steam locomotives (2-6-0, 2-6-2, 4-4-2, and 4-6-0 wheel arrangements) ruled main lines. Most cars were made of wood; a typical boxcar was 36 feet long and a typical freight train was 30 to 40 cars long.

1917: Railroads in the U.S. are nationalized under the United States Railroad Administration, continuing through World War I into 1920. The USRA established standard designs for locomotives and freight cars, many of which lasted through the steam era. 40-foot cars were common.

1920s: Railroad mileage peaked as railroads began abandoning light-density branch lines as highways expanded. Larger steam locomotives became common (2-8-2, 4-6-4).

1930s: Diesel switchers and passenger locomotives began entering service. Large, high-horsepower "modern" steam locomotives (2-8-4, 4-8-2, 4-8-4, 4-8-8-4) entered service. Most freight cars were steel; the 40-foot boxcar was the most common car type. Large-scale abandonment of light-density branch lines continued with the Depression.

1934: The first diesel streamliner, Burlington's stainless-steel fluted *Zephyr*, entered service. Others followed through the 1930s.

1939: Electro-Motive's streamlined FT (cab-unit body), the first successful road-freight diesel, made its debut.

1940s: Diesels began replacing steam locomotives in large numbers on both freight and passenger trains. Major builders included EMD, Alco, Baldwin, and Fairbanks-Morse.

1941: Alco introduced the RS-1, the first road-switcher design diesel locomotive.

1942-45: The War Production Board regulated locomotive production; only EMD was allowed to build road diesel locomotives. Alco and Baldwin were limited to diesel switchers, giving EMD a competitive advantage when wartime restrictions ended.

1948-49: The American Locomotive Co. (Alco) and Baldwin Locomotive Works built their last steam locomotives.

1949: EMD introduces its first road-switcher, the GP7. The road-switcher soon became more popular than streamlined cab-unit style diesels.

1950s: Diesels took over all mainline operations on Class I railroads by the end of the decade.

1955: Trailer Train (later TTX) was formed as a way for railroads to pool piggyback and intermodal equipment.

1959: General Electric introduced its first road diesel, the U25B. The company eventually became the leader in U.S. locomotive production.

1960s: Diesel locomotives and freight cars became larger and longer; six-axle road locomotives, 50- and 60-foot boxcars, and 89-foot piggyback flatcars and auto rack cars became common. Mechanical refrigerator cars took over from ice-bunker cars.

1967: The U.S. Postal Service canceled most rail mail contracts, which doomed most existing intercity passenger service.

1969: The New York Central and the Pennsylvania Railroad merged to form Penn Central.

1969: Alco exited the diesel locomotive manufacturing business.

1970s: Piggyback (trailer-on-flatcar) traffic increased, with solid trains becoming common, as did solid unit trains of coal hoppers and gondolas. 100-ton freight cars became the norm; covered hoppers took over for boxcars in grain traffic.

1971: Amtrak was formed, taking over most intercity passenger trains in the U.S.

1974: Railbox, a nationwide boxcar pool, was formed by several railroads in response to a shortage of general-purpose boxcars.

1975: REA Express (formerly Railway Express Agency), once the largest handler of package and express traffic, went out of business. Railroads exited the less-than-carload freight business.

1976: Conrail was formed with the merger of Penn Central and several other bankrupt Northeastern railroads.

1977: VIA Rail was formed in Canada and began operating that country's intercity passenger trains.

1980s: Most small-town depots with operators were eliminated, as railroads began to rely on radio communications instead of train orders handed to trains by operators. Double-stack container trains began appearing in large numbers.

1980: CSX was formed with the merger of Chessie System and Seaboard System (Seaboard Coast Line).

1982: Norfolk Southern was created by the merger of Norfolk & Western and Southern Railway.

1982: Cabooses were no longer required at the ends of trains, replaced by electronic EOT (end-of-train) devices; most cabooses were removed from service within a few years.

1987: General Electric passed EMD in U.S. locomotive production.

1995: Burlington Northern Santa Fe (now simply BNSF) was created by merger of Burlington Northern with the Atchison, Topeka & Santa Fe.

1996: Union Pacific absorbed Southern Pacific. The UP remains the longest-operating U.S. railroad, chartered in 1862 to build the eastern portion of the first transcontinental railroad.

2003: GE introduced its ES44 line of diesels, which—with design variants and upgrades, including the ES44AC—is still in production.

2004: EMD introduced its SD70ACe, which remained in production through 2014.

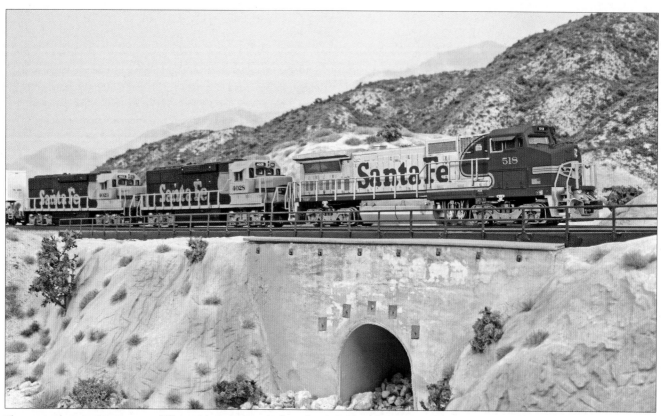

The second most common modeling scale is N. Ron Sipkovich models the Santa Fe's busy transcontinental main line through Cajon Pass as it existed in the early 1990s. Ron built the bridge from scratch. *Ron Sipkovich*

PS-1 design boxcar built by Pullman-Standard."

A **train set** refers to a prepackaged set of equipment that allows you to get trains running: usually a locomotive, some cars, a loop of track, and a power supply. A **layout** or **model railroad** refers to a more extensive setup, with trains, track, scenery, and details atop a permanent structure. (More on that in chapter 2.)

A **track plan** is a drawing that shows the location of all track, usually with other details such as structures, roads, rivers, and scenic elements. Many books of track plans have been published; you'll also find them in magazines and online.

Locomotives are the electrically powered models of prototype steam- or diesel-powered locomotives that lead trains. (They are sometimes referred to as *engines*, even though technically the engine is just a part of a locomotive.) **Rolling stock** refers to the freight cars, cabooses, and passenger cars that make up trains.

Track or **trackwork** is the combination of rails on ties that, like

prototype track, supports the trains. Unlike prototype track, model track also serves as the electrical path from the control system to the locomotive, meaning you have to be conscious of electrical circuits when laying (installing) track. The track rests upon **roadbed**, which provides an even, smooth surface for the track. (Chapter 8 provides more details.)

A **yard** is a group of tracks on model or prototype railroads where cars are sorted into trains by locomotives. Yards can vary in size from two or three tracks to dozens of tracks.

Scenery is anything that replicates real-life scenery and landscape, including grass, weeds, mountains, trees, roads, water, and rocks. The process of adding scenery is called *scenicking a layout*. Many books on scenery go into details on re-creating these effects, while chapter 10 gives a quick rundown of several.

Benchwork refers to the structure that supports the scenery, roadbed, and trains. It's most commonly assembled from wood components, such as dimensional lumber, plywood, and

hardboard, but sometimes features metal brackets and foam board. (See chapter 7 for details.)

Wiring is anything related to the electrical control of trains and accessories. The newest technology is Digital Command Control, which easily allows multiple operators to control several trains on the same track at one time. The traditional control method is direct current (DC) control using a power pack. (More on this in chapter 9.)

Scale and gauge

Models are built to a specific scale or proportion. *Scale* refers to a model's proportion compared to the real thing. For example, on an HO model (1:87 proportion), each dimension of the model is 1/87th of the real thing, so a 40-foot boxcar scales out to just over 5½".

The most common modeling scale today is HO, which is modeled by about 60 percent of hobbyists (see chapter 3). The next most common scale is N scale, at 1:160, which is modeled by about 20 percent of modelers (described in chapter 4).

Narrow gauge modeling is a popular subgroup of the hobby. Jim Hoffman based his HOn3 layout on Colorado's prototype Denver & Rio Grande Western and Rio Grande Southern of the late 1930s and early 1940s. *Peter Youngblood*

The majority of scale models are produced in HO and N scales, and both feature a tremendous variety of ready-to-run models and kits as well as accessories and ancillary items such as structures, vehicles, figures, and other details.

Other scales, although not as popular, also have devoted followings: O (1:48), S (1:64), Z (1:220), and various large scales with proportions ranging from 1:32 to 1:20, all of which share the same 45mm-gauge track.

Some products and techniques are tied to particular scales—a locomotive, freight car, or structure model, for example, is built to a specific scale. Other aspects of the hobby aren't scale dependent. Scenery materials and techniques, for example, can generally be used across various scales, and wiring practices (other than the specific power required) remains consistent through most scales.

Don't confuse scale with gauge. *Gauge* refers to the distance between the rails (prototype track has a gauge of 4'-8½"). Thus, an HO scale locomotive runs on HO gauge track, but the locomotive itself is not HO gauge.

Narrow gauge
North American railroads are built to a standard gauge of 4'-8½", a gauge that was widely used in the 1800s and eventually adopted as a national standard after the Civil War with the building of the first transcontinental railroad. Many earlier railroads were built to gauges between two and five feet.

Although most railroads built after that time were to standard gauge, some railroads were built with rails narrower than the standard—hence narrow gauge railroads. Most of these were three-foot-gauge (lines in Alaska, Colorado, New Mexico, California, Pennsylvania, and many small logging lines) or two-foot-gauge lines (Maine) built in rugged territory.

Famous three-footers included Colorado's Rio Grande Southern and Denver & Rio Grande Western, Alaska's White Pass & Yukon, and Pennsylvania's East Broad Top. Among Maine's two-foot lines were the Sandy River & Rangeley Lakes and the Bridgton & Saco River.

Most narrow gauge railroads were built with economics in mind: The theory being that it was more economical to build a railroad with smaller (narrower and shorter) locomotives and cars. Along with small equipment, curves could be tighter, grades steeper, and less earth and rock would have to be moved when building a line.

Although this proved true to a point, the smaller narrow gauge cars and trains couldn't move the amount of goods and products that standard gauge railroads could, and most were done in by competition from trucks as roads improved in the early 1900s. Almost all were abandoned or out of service by the 1940s. Today, several narrow gauge lines survive as tourist-carrying lines.

Although they represented just a tiny fraction of the North American rail system, narrow gauge lines have captured a disproportionately large amount of interest among modelers and railfans. The equipment they

Durango, Colo., was a hot spot for narrow gauge action into the 1940s. Here, a three-foot-gauge Denver & Rio Grande Western locomotive eases past the depot. *Ward Kimball*

used is interesting, and the scenery is beautiful, dramatic, and lends itself well to modeling. Most were relatively small operations, meaning a model railroader can model a good share of the equipment used by the real railroad. The small train sizes allow you to model trains of scale length—something difficult to do when modeling today's 110-car trains.

Because so many modelers choose to model narrow gauge railroads, a way was needed to designate models (locomotives, rolling stock, and track) based on those prototypes. The standard notation features the scale being modeled, followed by the letter *n* (indicating narrow gauge) and the gauge in feet. Thus, a model of a three-foot-gauge locomotive in S scale would be Sn3.

Remember that only the trains and track can be narrow gauge—structures, vehicles, and other items are in the scale being modeled.

For a detailed look at narrow gauge modeling and its possibilities, see Tony Koester's *Guide to Narrow Gauge Modeling* (Kalmbach, 2014).

Choosing a scale

Each scale has distinct advantages and disadvantages. In general, larger scales offer greater detail and finer modeling. Small scales allow you to have longer trains and more models in a given space, or let you build a model railroad in a compact space.

The larger the scale, the more visible the intricate details, and the easier it is to finely detail models. Many modelers simply like the heft of large (O, large scale, or even S scale) models. They generally operate extremely well, and it's easy to add lighting and sound effects.

A disadvantage is that these models take up a lot of space. A modern diesel locomotive is just over 70 feet long—a healthy 20" in O scale. Put a couple of these (or a large steam locomotive) on a train of 12 to 15 cars, and it will stretch the length of even a good-sized basement.

For some modelers, selecting a scale is an easy choice. For others, the decision can be difficult. If it's any consolation, some modelers who have been at it for 20 or 30 years are still trying to figure out their favorite scale.

Scale selection usually boils down to the amount of space you have, the availability of the models you're interested in, and the type of hobby activities you enjoy.

For example, if your available space is a 12 x 14-foot spare bedroom and your main interest is modeling a stretch of a modern Union Pacific main line with multiple towns, you're probably out of luck in O scale, pushing the limits in HO, but within reason in N scale. If your space is the same 12 x 14 feet, but you really want to re-create a highly detailed 1950s urban industrial scene with street trackage winding through it, then O or S would be fine choices.

Era and prototype

Many beginning model railroaders find themselves acquiring a great deal of equipment without any real rhyme or reason. Everything is new and exciting, so you may buy what looks interesting without considering prototypical accuracy and get a new, circa-2010 Union Pacific ES44 diesel, along with a couple of 1950s

Jason Klocke models branch line operations on his HO Chicago Great Western layout, complete with weeds overtaking the tracks in this circa-1960s scene. *Clark Propst*

Milwaukee Road passenger cars, a 1910-era steam locomotive, and some 1960s boxcars.

However, at some point, most modelers eventually stand back, take a deep breath, and dial in their focus a bit. You'll find that the more you learn about real railroads and the more you discover what your favorite areas of the hobby are, you'll find your interest gravitating toward a particular prototype railroad, certain types of equipment, and a general time period.

The ways in which modelers narrow their focus are varied. For some, re-creating the time period when they were young (or perhaps before they were born) has a nostalgic draw. It could be childhood memories or seeing a book, photos, or online video.

Before building your first layout, you certainly don't need to decide that you're modeling the Rock Island line through Estherville, Iowa, in September 1959. However, if you find yourself drawn to grain elevators and depots of the Midwestern or plains regions, late steam and early diesel equipment, and classic cars and trucks,

you can comfortably make your layout representational of a Midwestern scene of the 1940s or 1950s.

The number of prototype railroads has shrunk dramatically since the 1960s, as railroads continued to merge with each other and created larger and larger railroads. There are only five Class I (the largest division) railroads today, compared with more than 100 in the 1950s. For modelers and railfans, this means fewer road names appearing on the sides of locomotives and freight cars.

Whether your interest is in the past or present, as you learn about prototype railroads, you'll discover that each has its own personality. This is based on a railroad's size, region it traverses, equipment used, paint schemes, and primary business purpose. Finding a prototype that matches your interests can help you define what you want to model.

Style of railroading
If you look at a railroad map of the United States and Canada, you'll see thousands of lines crisscrossing each

other. Railroad mileage peaked in the 1930s and has been declining since, so by looking at a map from the 1940s or 1950s, you might discover routes you didn't know existed.

There are many types of railroad lines: main lines, secondary lines, branch lines, and industrial lines, all of which offer potential for modeling.

Main lines are a railroad's key routes that connect its major yards and cities. Main lines are built to high standards, with high-quality track and roadbed to withstand heavy traffic—several trains each way each day—and they often have lineside signals to regulate traffic. High-density main lines might see dozens of trains a day, and they can have two or more main tracks.

Main lines see both *through trains* (trains that travel the entire length of the line or between yards in major cities) as well as *way freights*, or *locals*— the trains that pick up and drop off cars at industries along the line.

Passenger traffic was found on most main lines into the 1960s, as most major main lines in the country hosted one or more passenger trains. As with

Weathered cars, graffiti, and weedy, chipped concrete all help set the scene on Lance Mindheim's highly detailed, modern-day HO industrial switching layout, set in Miami on the CSX. *Lance Mindheim*

freights, these could include named through trains that only stopped at major cities as well as locals that stopped at small intermediate stations.

Secondary main lines are routes that connect cities or interchange points but might not be the shortest routes between main points. They typically have less on-line business and pass through fewer or smaller towns. Secondary lines see less-frequent operations—perhaps one or two trains each way per day. In pre-Amtrak days, these routes were less likely to have regular passenger service. They are likely single-track lines, often without signals, and depots would be spaced farther apart as well.

Branch lines are routes that connect to a main line but either dead-end or meet another railroad at the other end. They can be short (a few miles to reach an industry or single town with multiple industries) or long, perhaps stretching 100 or more miles in granger territory to serve grain elevators in a dozen small towns.

Branch lines typically have lighter track that's not maintained to the same standards as a main line and require slower train speeds. Operations are less frequent, with many seeing a single train a day going out and back. Service was often cut back on these lines from the 1930s through the 1970s, and abandonments were common. Until then, service was sometimes cut back to weekly or as-needed basis.

Industrial lines can be branches of larger railroads or be independent railroads. These lines typically branch off a major railroad (or railroad yard), winding through major city industrial areas to serve several businesses in a relatively small area. Through the 1960s, these lines could often be found with tracks running in, along, and across city streets, in tight areas among buildings, and around tight curves.

Traction lines are also worth mentioning. On these electric railroads, locomotives draw power from a wire above the track. Traction lines include streetcars in cities, light-duty rural interurban lines (common especially in the Midwest through the 1930s), and heavy electric operations on conventional railroad main lines.

Freelancing railroads

You'll often come upon the term *freelancing* in model railroading. The term applies to modelers who have chosen to create their own imaginary railroad lines instead of following a specific prototype railroad. Doing this can be a great deal of fun, but doing it well requires a solid amount of prototype research and understanding of how real railroads work.

Freelancing can be done on many levels. Some modelers choose a specific prototype railroad but place it in cities or towns where it didn't actually go through, or sometimes add fictitious cities to an actual line. Another variation is to model a railroad beyond the era that it actually existed. For example, modeling the Great Northern as if it still existed today, instead of being merged into Burlington Northern in 1970.

Most commonly, freelancing involves creating a model railroad on a real map so that the towns, cities, and even routes are real—it's just the railroad that didn't actually exist. Modelers do this for a number

Traction railroads use an overhead wire to supply power to electric locomotives. Richard Abramson's HO scene represents the prototype New York, New Haven & Hartford's electric operations through Devon, Conn., in the early 1950s. *Richard Abramson*

of reasons: often they like several prototype lines, but can't make up their minds which one to follow, so they create a new line with the best features of their favorites.

Several famous model railroads have been freelanced, including Bill Darnaby's HO Maumee Route, based on several Midwestern lines, and Tony Koester's former HO Allegheny Midland, an Appalachian coal hauler.

To make freelancing believable, keep the name and theme of your railroad believable. It's usually wise to avoid cute, joke, or pun names, as they tend to get stale over time. The St. Louis & Western or Chicago, Denver & Pacific sound plausible and will wear better than the Onion Pacific or the Stinky Lake Southwestern.

Learning more

For more detailed information on any facet of the hobby, such as scenery, wiring, locomotives, or freight cars, check out books, videos, and online sources. Each chapter in this book includes an information box listing some of these sources.

To stay connected with the hobby, subscribe to a magazine or two, such as *Model Railroader* and *Railroad Model Craftsman*. If you're interested in today's prototype railroading, see *Trains* magazine, and for inspiration from bygone eras, check out *Classic Trains*.

There are historical societies for many past and present prototype railroads, and most offer books and periodicals. Do a web search for a railroad name and historical society to track them down. I strongly recommend joining one if you're interested in a specific railroad, as they often have a wealth of information that can't be found in other places.

Thousands of books have been published about specific railroads, locomotives, rolling stock, and operations. A quick web search will reveal what's out there. Even if books are out of print, check libraries, online auction sites, and dealers such as eBay, abebooks.com, and amazon.com. If it's been printed, it will be available somewhere.

More information

Guide to Narrow Gauge Modeling by Tony Koester (Kalmbach, 2014)

The Historical Guide to North American Railroads, Third Edition (Kalmbach, 2014)

Model Railroad Hobbyist online magazine (model-railroad-hobbyist. com)

Model Railroader magazine (mrr.trains.com)

The Model Railroader's Guide to Mountain Railroading by Tony Koester (Kalmbach, 2011)

Narrow Gauge and Short Line Gazette magazine (ngslgazette.com)

Railroad Model Craftsman magazine (whiteriverproductions. com)

The Railroad: What it Is, What it Does, Fifth Edition, by John H. Armstrong (Simmons Boardman, 2008)

Traction Handbook for Model Railroads by Paul and Steven Mallery (Carstens/White River Productions, 2008)

CHAPTER TWO

Layouts and track plans

Layouts can fill an entire basement, as with Gerry Albers' HO Virginian Railway. It's an around-the-walls design with multiple peninsulas that takes up a 40 x 50-foot area in his basement. The finished ceiling and walls, bright lighting, and nice floor all help make it a warm, inviting space. *Gerry Albers*

The ultimate goal for most modelers is to build a complete model railroad. There are many approaches to achieving this, including building layouts on small tables or shelves, or creating railroads that take up a spare room or even an entire basement. How you approach your layout is up to you.

Layout size

When first starting in the hobby, it's easy to become enamored of all the large, beautiful layouts showcased in hobby magazines. Understand that these layouts are often the culmination of decades of work for their builders. Most modelers build several smaller layouts before they embark on a large masterpiece.

When planning a first layout, it's always a good idea to start small. This gives you a chance to experience the many facets of layout building right away: benchwork, track laying, wiring, scenery, and detailing. It also gives you a chance to improve your skills and work on modeling. If you start on a huge project before your skills are ready, your enthusiasm will likely burn out before you even complete the benchwork—much less track and scenery.

Large layouts also represent significant investments in both time and money. When you start small, you can keep an eye on the future. Locomotives, rolling stock, and structures can all be moved forward to your next layout.

Even many experienced hobbyists continue to build small layouts. For some, it's a space consideration; for others, it's a matter of how much time and money they have to devote to the hobby. If you move frequently, building a large layout isn't practical, even if you have the space.

Large layouts also require multiple operators to run them. This can be a positive—especially if the social aspect of the hobby is important to you. If a large layout is your ultimate desire, by all means, keep reaching for and refining that goal until it is within your grasp.

Layout locations

Modelers have built layouts in a variety of locations, from suitcases to attics, showing that if you want a layout badly enough, you'll find a place for it. There's no such thing as a perfect layout area: all have positives and negatives, and you should be aware of these before diving into construction.

A key factor regardless of the location is that a space should be

Modelers often get creative to find layout space. Don Sauret finished an 11 x 19-foot attic space above his garage, working his HO layout under the roof slope and behind support posts at each end. *Don Sauret*

Layouts can coexist in family and living rooms. Greg Jones built his 1'-8" x 7'-0" layout in an old store display case and finished it with additional cabinetry. The N scale layout features an industrial switching design. *Lou Sassi*

Some modelers build layouts with two decks. By using the backdrop and shallow relief structures, it's possible to pack a lot of scenery and track into a narrow space. This is Tony Koester's HO Nickel Plate Road layout. *Tony Koester*

Dave Vollmer's N scale Pennsylvania Railroad is a small table-style design that fits in a small room. It's built on a pair of hollow-core doors (36" and 24" wide) with folding legs. Dave is in the Air Force, so he wanted a layout that could be easily moved. *Dave Vollmer*

Keith Jordan's L-shaped HO shelf-style switching layout fits perfectly around two walls of his upstairs studio. Each leg is about 8 feet long, with 12"-wide shelves. *Keith Jordan*

Model Railroader's Rice Harbor HO project layout (see MR January 2014) is built in two sections that connect down the middle. The harbor and carfloat at left fold down when not in use. *Bill Zuback*

comfortable and inviting. A room that's too cold, too hot, dimly lighted, smells musty, or is difficult to access is not be a place where you want to practice your hobby. After the initial excitement of having a layout, you won't be compelled to spend time in a place that's not comfortable.

Avoid spaces that experience extremes in temperature and humidity. Even if you think you can tolerate the conditions, your layout materials won't: benchwork lumber and other materials expand and contract, which leads to cracked scenery, kinked track, and poor operation.

Basements have been prime layout locations since the beginning of the hobby. The main advantage of a basement is ample space. Even in a small basement, it's usually possible to devote at least a small area to a layout, even if other space is needed for utilities, storage, and a recreation or family room. And if you're lucky enough to have a basement in a small ranch house, you might even have room for a more extensive model railroad.

Prepare the space before starting on your layout. First, make sure the basement is dry, taking care of any seepage or drainage issues. Run a dehumidifier in the summer to keep humidity down. By doing this, you'll experience fewer problems with wood expansion and contraction and have better air quality.

You don't need to completely finish a basement to make it suitable for a layout. Simply painting the floor and walls goes a long way toward brightening the space. The ceiling is also important. Open ceilings (often needed for plumbing and wiring access) tend to rain down dust as people walk on the floor above. Drop ceilings are relatively inexpensive and easy to install, and they cut down on dust and make the space brighter.

Lighting is important. Most unfinished basements are lit by a few bare bulbs. Replace these with multiple fluorescent fixtures, and if in doubt, add more light—you won't regret it.

Having carpeting will make it much more comfortable for standing, both when you are constructing your layout and while operating it. Carpet squares are an economical form of carpeting, and if you choose, you can keep them just on walkways and aisles.

Make sure your layout doesn't block access to utility components, including the furnace, water heater, utility meters, and electrical box. Be aware of local building and electrical codes and regulations regarding egress, room access, and construction materials.

Spare rooms are probably the next most common layout location. In these spaces, you may wish to add additional lighting, such as track lights. By going with an around-the-walls layout design, you can combine your layout with a home office, reading room, small shop, or bedroom.

Some modelers have been able to merge their hobbies with family activities and living spaces by incorporating layouts into family rooms, living rooms, or rec rooms. This is best done with shelf-style layouts or around-the-walls designs.

Attics and garages are also sometimes used for layouts, but these areas can require substantial work to make them usable. Providing proper temperature, eliminating dust, and creating easy access can all be challenges.

Table layouts

Many modelers immediately think "table" when planning a small layout. The 4 x 8-foot table—made popular because it's the most common size of a sheet of plywood—has spurred thousands of published track plans, and no doubt tens of thousands have been built.

Key advantages to a table layout are that table benchwork is easy and quick to build, you can fill a table with scenery in short order, and wiring is generally quite simple. A table layout can be a great way to learn about many aspects of the hobby in short order, and also be a great stepping stone to building a larger, more-detailed layout.

However, tables—especially the common 4 x 8—are far from ideal. In HO, that means having 18"- or, at

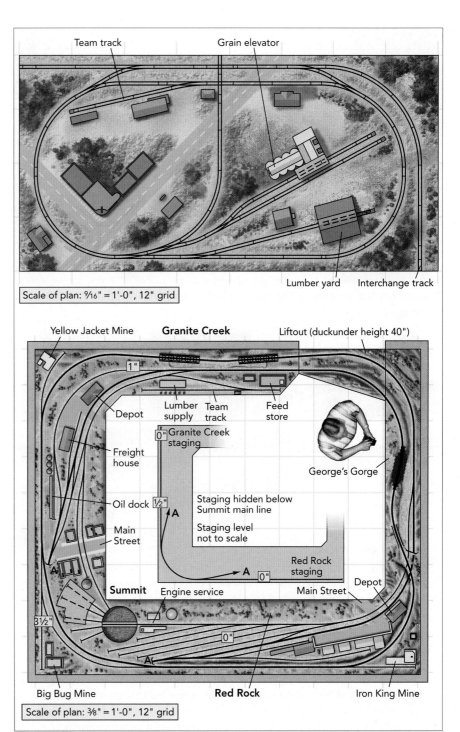

Scale of plan: 9/16" = 1'-0", 12" grid

Scale of plan: 3/8" = 1'-0", 12" grid

Track plans not only show the track but also structures, roads, rivers, and other details. The 4 x 8-foot HO plan (at top) is a simple loop with a passing track, several spur tracks, and two places where extensions could be added. The larger plan is designed to fit a 9 x 11-foot room. The plan is still a loop, but it goes twice around the walls and has a small hidden level for staging tracks.

most, 22"-radius curves, which are tight for long equipment. A bigger problem is that a 4 x 8 layout actually takes up a lot more space than 4 x 8 feet. Because a four-foot reach is simply too far to be practical, you need access to all four sides of a layout this size (or at least the two long sides and one end).

A two-foot aisle is workable but very tight, while three feet is better. This means that a 4 x 8 layout actually takes up a 10 x 14 space, and it leaves no room for much of anything else within that space.

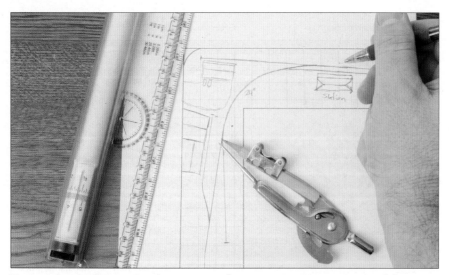

You can sketch plans on graph paper or, as here, on a computer printout of the layout space.

Trying plans (or portions of plans) in full scale is the best way to ensure that turnouts, structures, and other details will all fit in their intended spaces.

This makes it tough to get a 4 x 8-footer into a spare bedroom. It's still not a deal breaker, provided you have enough space (basement or larger rec room), but for a small room, consider planning an around-the-walls design or a narrower table in N scale (or a simple switching layout in HO) that can be placed against a wall. Chapter 7 explains how tables built on hollow-core doors have many advantages.

When considering a table layout, remember that any table or shelf wider than 30" requires access from both sides. You can stretch this to 36", but you'll probably regret it later when trying to work on scenery, uncouple a car, fix a derailment, or clean track at the back of the table.

Around-the-walls designs

The popularity of Digital Command Control, wireless throttles, and the ability to easily follow a train around a layout has led to a growth in around-the-walls layouts and designs. These are commonly called *walkaround designs* because you can always be with the train you're operating.

Shelf and around-the-walls layouts have many strengths. Shelves can be narrow but still allow much broader curves than do table-style layouts. You can have a relatively long mainline run even in a small bedroom, which makes large scales such as O workable in a small space. It's easy to include a backdrop along the wall to increase realism and make the layout seem larger than it really is.

Shelves also provide usable space under the layout for bookcases, entertainment centers, desks, workbenches, and storage, while leaving the center of a room open.

Shelves don't have to be wide to be effective. You can pack an amazing amount of detail in even a 12"-wide space. Having an 18" to 24" width allows multiple tracks with a lot of scenery and operational potential.

In larger spaces, such as basements, the around-the-walls style can be combined with peninsulas that jut into the room and extend the layout space and length of the main line. Some modelers go even further to get more layout in a given space by building two or three levels.

Benchwork can either be freestanding, which works well for apartments and condos, or fixed to the walls, as chapter 7 explains.

Challenges for these layouts include crossing doorways, where you must allow for either a lift-out, gate, or duckunder section. You also need to consider access to room features, including closets and windows, and—in basements—access to utilities.

Sectional and modular layouts

A layout that's built in multiple sections, designed to be easily taken down and reassembled in another location, is a *sectional layout*. A *modular layout* is a sectional layout with sections built to standard sizes and track specifications that can be interchanged with each other.

Modular model railroading has become quite popular since the 1980s. The theory is that not everyone has room for a big layout, but everybody has room to build a single module. Modules can then be brought together and combined to form large layouts for meets and train shows held in large areas.

By using modular design, groups aren't dependent on having everyone present for every meet—since modules are interchangeable. (If Bob and Doug can't make it to the gathering on Saturday, the layout is just assembled with two fewer modules.)

The leader in modular standards and layouts is Ntrak, an N scale group that began in the 1970s and now has thousands of participants. The basic Ntrak module has three tracks and is 4 feet long (see page 31; specifications can be found at ntrak.org). Ntrak layouts are common at train shows, and some have included huge layouts comprising several hundred modules.

A variation on Ntrak is oNeTRAK, which uses a single main track and Digital Command Control. (Specifications can also be found on the Ntrak website.)

Free-mo is an HO scale modular standard developed in the late 1990s. It emphasizes a free-form design with single track (double-track modules are also allowed). Track is centered, so modules can be placed in either direction. The modules can be any length and can curve. (See the organization's website, free-mo.org, for details.)

The ultimate in compact modular design is T-Trak (t-trak.org), which calls for small sections (just 12.2" long in N and 19.125" in HO) that sit atop separate tables, so no legs are required. Standards have been established for Z, N, HO, S, and O scale modules.

Track planning

Designing a layout or track plan is an art unto itself. Being able to plan trackwork, arranging it in a realistic manner, and combining it with structures, roads, and scenery can be a challenging task. For beginners, I highly recommend starting with a published track plan and making modifications as needed.

Regardless of size or scale, track plans follow a few basic patterns: loop, point to point, point to loop, or loop to loop. Loops are common for table layouts and around-the-walls designs, especially for those who simply like watching trains go by. Loops can also be hundreds of feet long if located in a large basement or room.

Point-to-point designs are favored by modelers who are pressed for space or who like to operate their layouts in the manner of prototype railroads. Large examples include basement empires that replicate several scale miles of track, with the main line

Loop plans

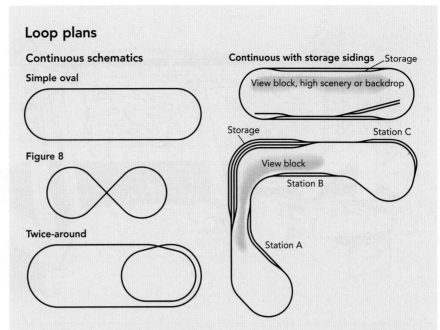

A loop is any design that lets a train run continuously in one direction, whether it's a simple oval on a table, a design that crosses over itself, or one stretched to an entire basement-filling, around-the-walls design with peninsulas. The longer the run, the more opportunities you have for adding towns, stations, passing sidings, industrial spurs, and other details. You can also hide a hidden storage or staging yard or tracks as in the plan at the lower right. This allows you to model realistic operations: for example, running a westbound (clockwise) passenger train over the layout, parking it in staging, and then bringing an eastbound (counterclockwise) freight train out and having it switch towns along the route.

Point-to-point plans

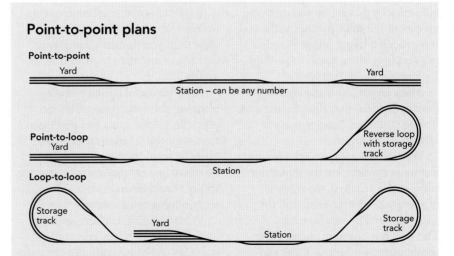

With point-to-point schematics, a train runs across the layout from end to end and passes through each scene or town once. The ends can simply terminate in yards or staging tracks, or have a loop at one end (point to loop) or both ends (loop to loop). The loops can also serve as staging tracks. Be aware that all reverse loops require special wiring to avoid short circuits (see chapter 9 for details).

Point-to-point designs include small switching layouts, such as Keith Jordan's (in photo on page 16), or basement railroads with main lines hundreds of feet long. These designs tend to be favored by modelers who want to run trains in a realistic manner, using timetables, train orders, and switch lists.

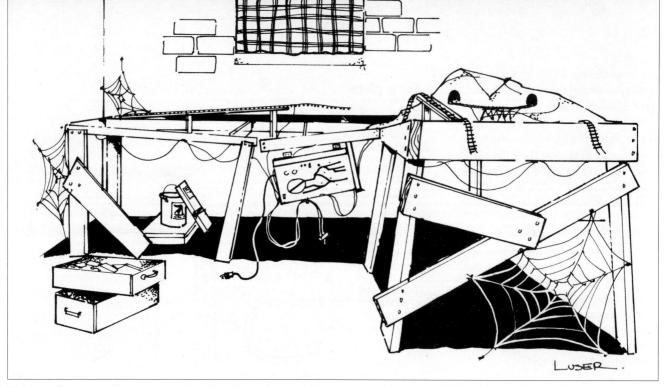

Trying to do too much too soon can lead to disappointment. Start small, work on your hobby skills, and expand your plans as you grow in the hobby. *Larry Luser illustration*

starting at a large yard in a city and passing through several small towns until it reaches another large yard.

Smaller versions include shelf-type switching layouts, which might be based on a single town or an industrial line in the city. Instead of running trains, the goal is switching the industries by picking up and dropping off cars in the same manner as the real thing. Such a layout might be only a few feet long along a wall or perhaps L-shaped around a corner.

Many layouts have staging tracks (usually hidden) that allow hiding and storing trains until they're ready to appear on the layout.

When developing a track plan, key factors to consider are the minimum curve radius required, the amount of space taken by turnouts, and the space required by parallel tracks. The next few chapters discuss curve requirements for various scales and types of equipment—it's critical that you stick to your minimum and not make curves tighter.

Graph paper is good for doodling plans. After drawing your overall space in ink, you can sketch in the track and other features. You can do this on a computer as well. This can be as simple as drawing the outline of your space using drawing software and printing

out copies of it, or you can add track, buildings, and other elements to the computer file.

The most common mistake beginners make when sketching a plan is including too many turnouts. These take a lot more space than you would think. A good way to get a feel for this is to lay out actual track components (or photocopies of turnouts) on a table until you find an arrangement that works and then transfer it to your sketch.

Another useful option is track-planning software. Atlas offers its planning software as a free download from its website (atlasrr.com). The software includes the company's extensive line of track components, the ability to add flextrack, and a function for trimming track sections.

Whatever your available space or modeling interests, the best way get started is to browse collections of published track plans, many of which are listed in the box at the right. Look for plans that match your interests, even if the size isn't what you're looking for. You can pull individual elements from several plans to get the overall design that matches your needs. Start small, work on your skill levels, and you'll soon be planning that large dream layout.

More information

45 Original Track Plans by Bernard Kempinski (Kalmbach, 2015)

101 More Track Plans for Model Railroaders (Kalmbach, 2011)

101 Track Plans for Model Railroaders (Kalmbach, 1956)

Compact Layout Design by Iain Rice (Kalmbach, 2015)

Free-mo (modular group and standards), free-mo.org

Mid-Size Track Plans for Realistic Layouts by Bernard Kempinski (Kalmbach, 2008)

Model Railroad Planning magazine (*Model Railroader* annual)

Model Railroading in Small Spaces, Second Edition, by Mat Chibbaro (Kalmbach, 2011)

Ntrak (modular group and standards), ntrak.org

Planning Your Model Railroad by Tony Koester (Kalmbach, 2014)

Shelf Layouts for Model Railroads by Iain Rice (Kalmbach, 2009)

Starter Track Plans for Model Railroaders (Kalmbach, 2012)

Track Design (Carstens/White River Productions 1996)

Track Planning for Realistic Operation, Third Edition, by John Armstrong (Kalmbach, 1998)

1

CHAPTER THREE

All about HO scale

HO (pronounced "aitch-oh") has been the most popular modeling scale since the 1950s, and for good reason. It has significant size, which allows for having a lot of detail on models. It's also small enough that you can fit a decent amount of modeling and operation into a relatively tight space, **1**. With a proportion of 1:87, a 40-foot boxcar in HO is 5½" long, **2**, and a scale mile is just over 60 feet.

HO scale allows for a lot of detail in a reasonable space. Here, an Amtrak train prepares to depart Sutherlynn Station on Bob Kingsnorth's freelanced layout. The lead locomotive is a Dash 8 from Atlas, the trailing unit is a Kato F40PH, and the Superliner passenger cars are from Walthers. *Bob Kingsnorth*

Detail evolution

HO scale models have come a long way in terms of both detail fidelity and operation. Both of the models shown here are GE U25Cs. The model at left was released by AHM in the mid-1960s; it was a good model for its time. The model at right is a current model produced by Rivarossi (which, in fact, was the company that made the original for AHM as well).

Note the many detail differences and improvements. The stamped-metal, unpainted handrails have become plastic, with fine cross-section and

accurate colors. Separate (or upgraded) details include the see-through grills (moldings on the old model), air hoses, uncoupling lever, speed-recorder cable (on the forward axle cap), radio antenna, air horn (a style now accurate for the Burlington), number-board numbers, windshield wipers, cab sunshades, model-designation plate, nose handrails, fuel filler, window gaskets, and improved brake wheel. The paint job is better, both in accuracy and the sharpness of the lettering, herald, and stripes.

The new model has a body-mounted knuckle coupler, replacing the old truck-mounted horn-hook, and wheels with RP-25 flanges replacing the old deep flanges (found on some European-made equipment into the 1970s).

What's not as apparent are the internal improvements. The old AHM "growler" motor had a speed range of 6 to 170 scale mph (per an early magazine review). The new model has a smooth-running enclosed motor, with factory-installed Digital Command Control and sound.

HO scale evolved from its size compared to O: It's about half of O, thus HO. The scale was first developed in the United Kingdom, which explains why it is based on a metric size of 3.5mm equaling a foot. The scale didn't gain popularity in the UK, where OO scale (slightly larger, at 4mm to the foot, and 1:76 proportion) became dominant. Although a few companies offered American-prototype OO models, that scale never caught on in great numbers. Instead, it was HO in the 1930s that was adapted in the United States by several manufacturers.

Walthers issued its first HO scale catalog in 1937, and product availability continued growing though the 1940s and 1950s. The scale quickly became popular with scale model railroaders, who found they could fit more modeling into a given area compared to O or S scales.

As more modelers were drawn to the scale, manufacturers such as Globe (later Athearn), Varney, Bowser, Lindberg, Mantua, Tyco, Roundhouse/ Model Die Casting, and Revell all

expanded their product lines. Along with trains, significant numbers of structure kits and detail parts also became available.

HO today

HO remains the most popular modeling scale largely because current models run beautifully and are accurately detailed to a level beyond what could be purchased even 10 years ago.

The biggest evolution in the past decade has been the growth in high-quality ready-to-run (RTR) locomotives and freight cars. Through the 1990s, HO was still regarded as a "modeler's" scale, in that most high-quality freight cars and structures were available only in kit form (and "serious" modelers tended to scoff at easy-to-assemble, "shake-the-box" kits). Locomotives were available in ready-to-run form, but modelers often had to add finishing details such as grab irons and handrails. Fine details (and railroad-specific variations) were often left to the modeler, using aftermarket parts such as windshield wipers,

rooftop beacons, radio antennae, horns, alternate headlights, and air hoses.

Buying a ready-to-run diesel locomotive having prototype-specific details, paint, and lettering meant buying a limited-run brass model at an investment of at least $300 (and more for steam locomotives).

The late 1990s saw an increase in detail found on locomotive models. The idea was novel—a plastic model with loads of detail, matched to specific prototypes, but with a bigger price tag and available in limited runs only. The models sold well, and the idea soon became common among makers of high-end locomotive models.

As advances in Digital Command Control (DCC) increased its popularity (more on that in chapter 9), locomotive manufacturers responded first by offering models with prewired sockets, allowing plug-equipped decoders to be added without having to solder connections, and then by selling locomotives equipped with decoders.

Locomotive makers have kept up with technology, and today's models are available not only with multifunction decoders and lighting effects, but with sound decoders that offer a full range of effects, including horn and engine sounds matched to specific prototype locomotives, **3**.

Perhaps the biggest step forward in the RTR revolution came from Kadee, which caused quite a stir in 1997, when it introduced its first HO model, a ready-to-run 40-foot PS-1 boxcar, **4**. At the time, an RTR freight car meant a low-quality, "train-set" car, often with with poor detailing and unrealistic paint and lettering schemes.

Kadee's model was notable for several reasons. First, it was a ready-to-run model with superb detail, including separate finely molded grab irons, a see-through grid running board, detailed brake gear and underbody, and variations to match specific prototype cars (including brake wheel style, door type, and door size). It was (and still is) available in road names accurate for that particular version of the car.

It was equipped with Kadee knuckle couplers—notable in a time when most models still had horn-hook couplers—and metal trucks and wheelsets, all features which at the time were only available in high-end plastic kits.

Also notable was the price tag: about $30, almost double what a high-quality plastic kit cost at the time (and close to the cost of many diesel locomotives). Many predicted that this pricing would never work, but the car was a success. Most other manufacturers followed suit, first by offering their kits in assembled versions, then—if they hadn't already done so—by upgrading to metal wheelsets and knuckle couplers. Today, rolling stock kits have become rare, and ready-to-run cars are the standard.

Passenger cars have also followed suit, from generic RTR cars with no interior detail, painted in many railroads' schemes, to entire trains based on specific prototypes, with interior details, upgraded wheels and couplers, and—in many cases—lighting, **5**.

The art of building models is not dead by any means. Kits are still available for many freight cars, including craftsman-style resin kits

2 A 40-foot boxcar in HO is about 5½" long. This is a ready-to-run model from InterMountain.

3 Locomotive models have a lot packed inside their shells. Athearn's HO scale model of a modern GE ES44AC includes a DCC sound decoder and speakers above the motor and flywheels, with weights taking up the remainder of the interior. *Bill Zuback*

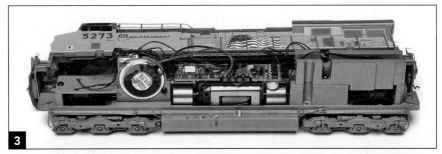

4 When introduced in the late 1990s, Kadee's HO ready-to-run 40-foot PS-1 boxcar was revolutionary for its level of detail and prototype fidelity.

5 Many companies have released passenger cars matching specific prototypes (or entire trains). This Walthers model represents a Budd Vista-Dome 48-seat coach as built for Great Northern's *Empire Builder*.

6

Running long cars on tight curves—in this case, Walthers 89-foot piggyback cars on 18"-radius sectional track—will result in derailments and poor operation.

7

Couplers can be manually uncoupled by placing an uncoupling tool, like this one from Accurail, or a small screwdriver between the knuckles and twisting.

8

The horn-hook coupler was standard on ready-to-run and kit-based rolling stock and locomotives into the 1990s. They look unrealistic and operate poorly.

based on specific prototypes. Older freight car kits are still available and offer potential for detail upgrades. Many buildings come in assembled versions, but kits—including highly detailed plastic models—still rule the structure market, giving modelers the chance to build and customize models.

Layout planning
Restrictions in layout planning for any scale are largely based on curves— namely, the tightest-radius curve that can be used with the equipment that

you're planning to operate. In HO, the de facto standard for sectional track has long been 18" radius, making a complete loop 36" wide. Since a good rule of thumb is to allow at least 6" between track and the edge of a layout, this means a minimum 4-foot-wide table (as on a typical 4 x 8-foot layout) for HO layouts.

With 18"-radius track, short equipment works best: four-axle diesels, small steam locomotives, and 40- and 50-foot freight cars. Six-axle diesels and 60-foot cars usually work, but their ends overhang the track and do not look very realistic on curves. Longer equipment, such as modern diesels, steam locomotives with four or more driving axles, 89-foot piggyback flatcars, auto racks, and passenger cars, usually presents too many operational problems to work well, **6**. Truck rotation and car-end overhang may interfere with the couplers and cause derailments.

Broader curves look much better, and they allow you to run longer locomotives and cars. Sectional track is widely available in 22" radius; use this instead of 18" wherever possible.

Ideally, try even broader curves if you can; flextrack allows you to lay track of any radius needed (see chapter 8).

As chapter 2 discusses, table-style layouts take up much more room than is sometimes apparent when you add the access space needed around all sides of any table wider than about 30". In HO, this means to look beyond a table and consider a shelf or around-the-walls style layout instead. This is especially true if your preference is toward mainline railroading, passenger operations, or modern railroads with long freight cars.

Couplers
Automatic knuckle couplers are now standard on all new HO models. These resemble and work similarly to prototype couplers, but models have a sprung knuckle that allows cars to be simply pushed together to couple. Uncoupling can be manual, by inserting an uncoupling tool or thin screwdriver between the knuckles and twisting, **7**, or automatic, by using a between-the-rails or under-track magnet. By pausing the couplers over the magnet, the magnet pulls the steel uncoupling pins (the curved pieces under the coupler) apart and opens the knuckles.

Some modelers use the magnetic uncoupling feature, especially on spurs and secondary tracks where cars are typically dropped off and picked up, but generally not on main lines, where cars can accidentally uncouple if a train slows down over a magnet. Many modelers today remove the pins for greater realism; others paint them dark gray or black to represent air hoses.

Kadee was the pioneer in developing realistic knuckle couplers, and its Magne-Matic line of couplers has been available since the 1950s. Into the 1990s, it was virtually the only brand of knuckle couplers available, and they were only available as aftermarket items.

Until that time, all cars were factory equipped with the horn-hook coupler, **8**. These couplers operated as poorly as they looked. Horn-hook couplers coupled easily but were difficult to uncouple, and because of their design, pushing strings of cars

9 Remove the coupler box lid to replace the couplers. This is a Kadee no. 158 whisker-spring coupler (left) and no. 5 coupler with separate bronze spring (right) in Accurail boxcars.

10 Kadee's coupler height gauge is invaluable in ensuring that all cars on your layout are mounted at the same height. The uncoupling pin should clear the base on the gauge.

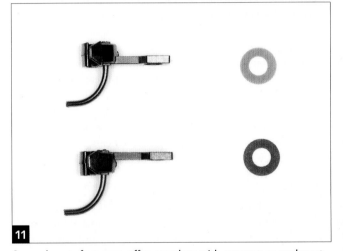

11 Several manufacturers offer couplers with overset or underset shanks. *Jim Forbes*

12 Replacement metal wheelsets include Kadee code 110 with scale 36" wheels (in an Accurail truck, left) and narrow-tread Reboxx code 88 (33") wheelsets (right).

with horn-hook couplers could lead to derailments.

By that period, most serious modelers had adopted the Kadee coupler as standard. Kadee continues to offer a full line of knuckle couplers, including smaller, scale-size versions that have become very popular. After Kadee's original patents expired in the late 1990s, other companies began offering knuckle couplers, including Accurail Accumate, Athearn (McHenry), and Bachmann E-Z Mate II. Couplers are available with a variety of shank lengths to fit specialized installations.

Many modelers simply keep the couplers that come with equipment; others standardize on a specific brand.

Most operate well, but you may notice occasional cross-compatibility issues with couplers from different manufacturers, where they balk at coupling or uncoupling.

Most cars are now equipped with body-mounted couplers, and longer cars often have some type of extended draft gear that allows the coupler shank to rotate on sharper curves. Many older HO cars (especially low-quality models) had truck-mounted couplers. Although truck-mounted knuckle couplers generally operate well, they aren't realistic—they make it difficult to add uncoupling lever and air hose details.

Changing couplers is usually just a matter of removing the existing coupler box lid, which is held by a small screw,

clip, or press-in pin, and placing a new coupler and spring in place, **9**. Make sure the coupler shank moves freely from side to side with no binding. If it binds, check for stray plastic or other material, or find a different coupler to drop in.

To operate properly, all couplers on your layout must be mounted at the same height. Mismatched couplers will uncouple, especially on hills or uneven track, and the uncoupling pins on low-hanging couplers can snag on turnouts and crossings, which can derail cars and damage equipment.

Kadee makes a coupler height gauge that should be a standard tool for any HO scale modeler, **10**. Before placing any car or locomotive in service, check it against the gauge on a test track. The

This 2-10-4 steam locomotive from Broadway Limited Imports is typical of today's HO steam locomotive offerings. It's equipped with DCC, sound, and a smoke unit, and it features lots of detail including a crew in the cab. *Bill Zuback*

top of the coupler should match the top of the coupler on the gauge, and the uncoupling pin should clear the lower pad.

(Don't place a standard metal Kadee no. 205 gauge on live track, or you'll cause a short circuit. Kadee makes an insulated version of the gauge, no. 206, which is safe to use on powered track.)

If a coupler is too low or too tall, you can replace the coupler with a new one having an underset or overset shank, **11**. (Kadee and other manufacturers offer them.) Save the original coupler for future use in another car.

Wheels and trucks

A *truck* includes the sideframes (typically molded in Delrin or other self-lubricating engineering plastic) as one piece, with two sideframes spanned by a bolster, and wheelsets. A *wheelset* is each assembly of two wheels on an axle. Model wheelsets typically have needlepoint axles that rest in pockets in the sideframes. Most are very free-rolling.

Models come with several wheel/wheelset material combinations. Some wheelsets are molded as a solid piece of plastic, some have plastic wheels mounted on metal needlepoint axles, others have metal wheels on plastic axles, and some have metal wheels (one side insulated) on metal axles.

When getting started, you're usually fine with keeping the factory-equipped wheels. Many modelers eventually choose to replace wheelsets for both appearance and operational reasons. One consideration is metal wheels vs. plastic ones. I always opt for metal. Metal wheels stay cleaner, and they help track stay cleaner (they effectively polish each other during operation). Over time, plastic wheels will build up gunk on wheel treads, which need to be cleaned. Metal wheels are also heavier, which lowers a car's center of gravity and helps it track better, **12**.

Another issue is size. Most wheelsets have wheel treads .110" wide (code 110). A recent development is the move toward wheels with .088"-wide treads (code 88). Also called *semi-scale* wheels, these look more realistic but aren't quite as narrow as the real thing. (A group devoted to fine-scale modeling, Proto:87, does this; special track is also required—see proto87.com.) Some models come from the factory with code 88 wheels, but they're still largely an aftermarket item.

Several manufacturers offer replacement metal wheelsets, including Kadee, ReBoxx, InterMountain, and Walthers Proto. You'll find references to scale 33"- or 36"-diameter wheels. The 36" wheels are appropriate for 100-ton and 110-ton capacity cars (modern jumbo covered hoppers,

gondolas, and tank cars). Use 33" wheels on 70-ton, 50-ton, and lighter cars (most modern boxcars and most cars before the early 1960s).

Swapping wheelsets is a simple matter of flexing the sideframes apart, removing the old wheels, and snapping the new ones in place.

Locomotives

Today's high-quality HO diesel and steam locomotives are amazing in their level of detail, accurate paint schemes, operational quality, and factory-equipped sound and light features, **13**. These include lines from Athearn Genesis, Atlas Master, Bowser Executive, Broadway Limited Imports, Fox Valley Models, InterMountain, Kato, MTH, Rapido, Rivarossi, and Walthers Proto.

Other lines feature models that still operate well, but with a lower level of detail and without factory-installed DCC and sound. These include Atlas Trainman, Bowser Traditional, and Walthers Trainline and Mainline. Also, if you shop around, you'll find many models built in the last 20 years that are fine quality but perhaps not equipped for DCC.

Visually, the biggest evolution has been the change from molded-on details (grab irons, fans, grills, etc.) to separately added details or much better molded details. (See the sidebar on page 22 for a comparison.)

Code 83 track, like the Atlas sectional piece at left, has a more-realistic rail height and better spike and tie-plate detail. Code 100 track, like the brass section at right, has oversize rail and heavy, unrealistic spike detail.

Blackstone offers many outstanding HOn3 models, including the tank car at left. The standard gauge InterMountain car at right provides a size comparison.

Through the 1990s, superdetailing was a popular subset of the hobby, with aftermarket companies like Cal-Scale, Detail Associates, Details West, Cannon, and Precision Scale, along with paint and decal makers, offering parts for customizing models to match specific prototype locomotives.

Nowadays, high-end models include many of the features that once had to be purchased and applied separately, including grab irons, fans with separate fan blades, antennas, beacons, strobe lights, ditch lights, windshield wipers, door latches, fuel fillers, headlight housings, etched-metal grills, m.u. housings and cables, and uncoupling levers. Trucks now feature better depth of details, with separate journal covers, hangers, dampers, and brake shoes.

Getting inside a modern model can be tricky, but—for the most part—there's no maintenance to be done, short of adding or replacing a DCC decoder. If you must do so, check the owner's guide carefully. Diesel shells are usually held in place by hidden tabs or screws mounted from under the frame.

Diesel locomotives usually have a heavy metal frame with the motor, flywheels, and drive mechanism mounted atop it, with a circuit board on top of that. Cabs often have interior details, including seats, control stands, and sometimes figures.

Most locomotive models today are powered by small enclosed, low-current-draw motors that operate smoothly and at extremely low speeds. A driveshaft at each end of the motor is connected to a universal joint and gears that drive axles on each truck.

For steam, the motor is in the boiler, with a driveshaft at the front end powering the drivers. Electronics are typically in the tender, with a mini cable or plug that must be connected between it and the locomotive.

(Chapter 6 provides more details on locomotives, and chapter 9 provides details on DCC and other control systems.)

Older locomotive models are often available at bargain prices, and—depending upon your needs, modeling level, and control system (and willingness to learn to add decoders)—can be a good choice.

Track

HO scale boasts a wide range of track products, including sectional track with and without molded-plastic ballast, turnouts of many sizes, crossings in several angles, as well as flextrack with simulated wood or concrete ties.

Code 83 nickel-silver track (rail .083" tall) has become the standard for HO. It's durable, easy to cut and shape, and looks much better than code 100 (.100") track, which was the most common size through the 1980s, **14**. Avoid track with brass rail, which was also common then, as it requires

more frequent cleaning than nickel-silver. (Chapter 8 provides details on choosing and laying track.)

HO narrow gauge

The most common variation is HOn3 (HO scale with three-foot-gauge track), following Colorado prototypes (see photo on page 9), logging railroads, and Pennsylvania lines. Manufacturers of HOn3 products include Blackstone Models (cars and locomotives, along with track/roadbed sectional track), Durango Press, and Mountain Model Imports, **15**.

Micro Engineering offers code 40, 55, and 70 flextrack, turnouts, and track components, and Peco and Shinohara make code 70 track. Micro-Trains has freight car trucks and wheels.

Another variation is modeling prototype two-foot-gauge railroads (primarily found in Maine through the 1930s) by using N gauge track, which scales to 30" in HO. The resulting combination is called HOn2½ or HOn30. (Check out hon30.org for information on suppliers and past published articles.)

More information
HOn3 Annual (White River Productions, published annually)
Rebuilding a Layout from A-Z by Pelle K. Søeborg (Kalmbach, 2012

1

CHAPTER FOUR

Introduction to N scale

Today's N scale models feature outstanding detail, and many modelers combine these models with fine scenery to create realistic scenes. This view of two lightning-striped New York Central F units leading a freight train is on Ed Nottage's layout, set in the summer of 1957. *Brooks Stover*

When N scale first appeared, in the early 1960s, it was largely a gimmick. Few models were available; couplers, wheels, and other details were oversized and clunky; and locomotives often didn't run well—*Stop* and *Full speed ahead* were the basic settings for many models. Fast-forward to today: modern N scale models are beautifully detailed and run smoothly, and modelers have a broad range of choices for trains and accessories, **1**.

The reason N scale came to exist was a quest for smaller-than-HO models to fit in small spaces. By 1960, HO was by far the dominant modeling scale. At the time, the smallest modeling scale was TT (1:120), which—although reasonably popular in Europe—never caught on with U.S. modelers or manufacturers, possibly because it wasn't enough of a size reduction compared to HO (1:87).

Several companies toyed with smaller model trains (mainly European prototypes) ranging from 1:150 to 1:200, but in 1962, the Arnold Company (Arnold Rapido) brought out American prototype models in 1:160, which would eventually be known as N scale. There wasn't much: an F unit, a Baldwin diesel, and a couple of freight cars. Although crude by today's standards, they were enough to attract the interest of U.S. modelers interested in the possibilities of modeling in a smaller scale. The size is just over half of HO: a 40-foot boxcar is 3" long, **2**, and a scale mile is 33 feet.

Through the 1960s, N scale increased in popularity, with Trix (Minitrix), Atlas, Aurora (Postage Stamp train sets), MRC, Peco, Con-Cor, and others introducing products by the end of the decade.

Popularity was enhanced in 1972 when Kadee (now Micro-Trains) introduced its line of freight cars, which featured N scale versions of Kadee's Magne-Matic couplers. Kadee's cars had higher levels of detail than most earlier offerings, they ran beautifully, and they showed that better, more realistic models were possible on small models.

Along with couplers, Kadee sold its trucks with truck-mounted couplers separately as well, so it was easy for modelers to upgrade other makers' cars, which greatly improved operating reliability in the scale.

By the early 1970s, N was accepted as a "serious" modeling scale, with a wide range of products, modelers building large and small layouts, and modeling efforts being showcased regularly in magazines such as *Model Railroader* and *Railroad Model Craftsman*.

N scale's proportion is 1:160, meaning this 40-foot Micro-Trains Line boxcar is 3" long.

Kato's modern EMD SD70ACe diesel is an example of the high-quality locomotive models being offered in N scale.

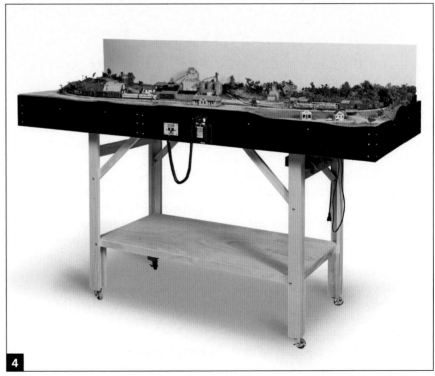

You can fit a lot of railroad in a small space with N scale. The Red Oak layout is just 3'-0" x 6'-8", but includes a full oval, several staging tracks behind the backdrop, and multilevel scenery with several industries on the front side of the backdrop. It was built by the *Model Railroader* staff and featured in the January 2015 issue. *Bill Zuback*

A spare room or basement can produce an empire in N scale. Tom Basterash's layout fits in a 10 x 11-foot room, but looks much larger. The main line is 65 feet long (about 2 scale miles). *Tom Basterash Jr.*

Being able to model dramatic scenes and realistically long trains are strengths of N scale. Dan Lewis built this scene on his Milwaukee Road layout to represent Montana in 1953. He digitally added the smoke to the Bachmann Spectrum locomotives. *Dan Lewis*

Today, N scale's offerings—although not quite as broad as those in HO—cover most areas, with a wide range of diesel and steam locomotives and rolling stock as well as track, structures, and accessories.

The quality of high-end models in N scale today is outstanding, **3**. Locomotives and rolling stock have many separately added details, with many models matching specific prototypes. Running capability of the locomotives equals that of HO, with good speed control, and locomotives are available with factory-equipped Digital Command Control (DCC) and sound.

Two hobby interests spurred the rapid growth and sustained popularity of N scale: the ability to get a lot of modeling into a relatively small space (great for apartment dwellers and others having limited space), and the ability to model significantly long stretches of main lines in large spaces (and run realistically long trains).

Layout planning

As in HO, restrictions in layout planning are based on the minimum radius of track curves. The standard minimum radius for most sectional N scale track is 9¾" (meaning a

full loop of track is 19½" across). Depending upon the brand and track line, you'll also find 10", 11", 12½", 13¾", 15", 16¼", 19", 21¼", and 25" radius track sections.

Although you can run quite a bit of equipment on 9¾" curves (four-axle diesels, small steam locomotives, and cars up to 50 feet), you'll have more choices—and trains will look much better—on broader curves. For modern six-axle diesels and long piggyback cars and auto racks, use curves at least 15", and broader if possible.

In N scale, you can fit a reasonable table-style layout with a complete oval of track and a few spur tracks in a 24" x 48" space, and even more with a slightly larger table, **4**. Unlike in HO, you can locate this table against a wall (the 24" reach is reasonable without rear access) and save space.

You can also mount such a layout on a shelf along a wall, again including a full oval (or turnback loops at each end) without the need for a separate peninsula or rear access.

For shelf-style layouts, shelves can be quite narrow—a shelf 6" wide can easily carry a single track between towns, and modeling a town or industry with multiple tracks is possible in a space 12" wide. Remember that aisles should be just as wide as any other scale.

You can have long mainline runs, expansive scenery, and multiple towns even in small spare bedrooms, **5**, and a basement will provide even more modeling opportunities, **6**.

Ntrak and other modules

Modular and sectional railroading (yes, there's a difference) has become popular in several scales, and N scale deserves much of the credit. A sectional layout is any model railroad built in multiple pieces (usually table-like pieces) that can be taken apart and reassembled. Many clubs use a sectional approach, which can be done if a group doesn't have a permanent layout or wants a layout that can be easily moved to take to shows. Some modelers choose to build their home layouts in sections, often to make it easier to save a layout when moving to a new home.

With a sectional layout, individual sections are designed to fit in specific locations: if the order is section A, B, C, and D, it won't work if section C is missing since B can't be joined to D.

A modular layout is a sectional layout, but it has sections that are interchangeable with each other, and each module is built to specific standards and specifications. This way, a layout can be set up with as many modules as are available.

Modular railroading got its start in the early 1970s with Ntrak, a standard that is still popular today, **7**. An Ntrak module is 2 x 4 feet (although other modules are allowed in 2-foot increments), with three tracks that run along the front of each module. Additional tracks are allowed on individual modules. Modules are clamped together and connected electrically with universal plug-and-socket connectors.

Many local clubs are based on Ntrak standards, with individual members building their own module or modules (corner modules are often owned by the club itself), **8**. Multiple clubs and groups often get together at large meets, such as regional and national conventions, train shows, and other events, to combine their modules into large layouts—sometimes with hundreds of modules involved. (You can find a list of standards and specifications on ntrak.org.)

Other types of module standards have since been established, including oNeTrak, a single-track version of Ntrak modules using DCC (see details on the Ntrak website), and T-Trak (t-trak.org), which is based on small, table-top dioramas, with standards in Z, N, HO, S, and O scales, **9**.

Couplers and wheels

Until the late 1990s, N scale locomotives and rolling stock (other than Micro-Trains) came equipped with Rapido couplers, **10**. As with the HO horn-hook, these couplers neither operate nor look particularly well. They pivot up and down, with an angled face allowing one to slide up and over another to couple together—usually

7 Jim Kelly built an Ntrak module that represents the Santa Fe near Caliente, Calif., in the 1980s. *Jim Forbes*

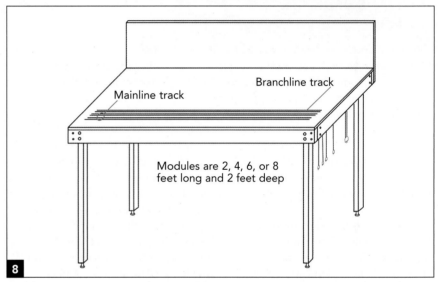

Mainline track

Branchline track

Modules are 2, 4, 6, or 8 feet long and 2 feet deep

8 Ntrak modules are simple to build: a piece of plywood atop a box frame, plus four legs and a backdrop. Dimensions and full specifications can be found at ntrak.org.

9 Ttrak modules are designed to sit atop a flat table. Pelle Søeborg built a rural scene on his module as part of an MR Video Plus project.

10

The Rapido coupler was standard on most N scale rolling stock and locomotives into the 1990s.

11

N scale knuckle couplers include those from Kato, Athearn, and Micro-Trains (left to right).

12

You can mount Micro-Trains or other couplers directly to car ends, although you may have to add styrene mounting plates to some types of cars, as Jim Kelly did on this Atlas covered hopper. *Jim Kelly*

13

These Micro-Trains trucks are shown, from left, with M-T deep-flange plastic wheels, M-T shallow-flange plastic wheels, and InterMountain metal wheelsets.

quite easily. Uncoupling, however, is difficult, requiring one to be lifted back up over the other—almost impossible to do without lifting the entire end of a car.

Most serious modelers swapped them for Magne-Matic automatic knuckle couplers, making Magne-Matic the de facto standard in N scale. The late 1990s saw a flurry of additional knuckle couplers on the market, and soon all N locomotives and freight cars were being offered with knuckle couplers, **11**.

More information

Building a Model Railroad Step by Step, Second Edition, by David Popp (Kalmbach, 2012)

N Scale magazine, nscalemagazine.com

N Scale Railroading magazine, nscalerailroadn.com

N Scale Railroading, Getting Started in the Hobby, Second Edition, by Marty McGuirk (Kalmbach, 2009)

Ntrak (modular group), ntrak.org

As in HO, most of these work well, but you may discover compatibility issues when mating various brands. You don't have to worry about this right away, but some modelers choose to standardize with one brand. Current knuckle couplers include the Accumate (on Atlas and other cars), Kato, and McHenry (Athearn cars). Other manufacturers use these couplers or Magne-Matics under license.

Magne-Matics and other brands are available as separate items, in various shank lengths and mounting configurations, and mounted on trucks. Micro-Trains offers conversion instructions for many manufacturers' cars and locomotives on its website (micro-trainsline.com).

Most rolling stock was once equipped only with truck-mounted couplers, but many cars (and almost all locomotives) now have body-mounted couplers. You can also fit body-mounted couplers on older cars if you choose, **12**.

Micro-Trains makes a coupler height gauge (no. 1055) that all N scalers should have. Because of their small size, proper alignment and height of couplers are especially important in N scale.

A lot of older N scale equipment had wheels with deep flanges. These will bump the ties on most code 55 track. Micro-Trains has long offered its cars with sets of both shallow- and deep-flange wheels—there's really no reason not to use the more realistic shallow-flange wheels, **13**. As with HO, replacement metal wheelsets are available from Atlas, BLMA, ExactRail, Fox Valley Models, InterMountain, and NorthWest Short Line.

Locomotives

Most N scale diesel locomotives feature an injection-molded styrene shell, with a mix of molded and separately applied details, **14**. This slides over a metal chassis. Inside this, a small motor with flywheel drive gears power all axles on both trucks.

All wheels should be used for electrical pickup. A circuit board on top of the chassis contains wiring connections, LED headlights, and—if so equipped—a DCC decoder, **15**.

Steam locomotives are similar, but the motor (inside the boiler) powers the drivers. Electronics are often located in the tender, with small

14

Bachmann's model of EMD's 1940s-era NW2 switcher shows off the quality typical of today's N scale models—with an injection-molded styrene shell, painted handrails, and fine lettering (such as builder's plate). *Bill Zuback*

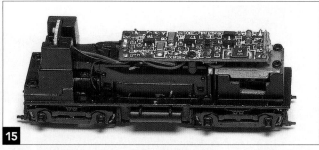

15

The circuit board inside the NW2 includes a DCC decoder. The headlights at front and rear are tiny surface-mount LEDs. *Bill Zuback*

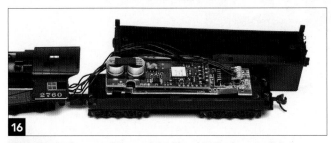

16

Most steam locomotive models, like this Bachmann 2-8-4, carry electronics in the tender—in this case, a DCC decoder and downward-facing speaker (in the floor). *Bill Zuback*

17

This Milwaukee Road baggage car from Fox Valley Models features sharp lettering and separately applied grab irons, underbody detail, end diaphragms, and roof detail.

jumper wires connected by a miniature plug and socket, **16**.

There's very little reason, short of adding or replacing a decoder, for getting inside a locomotive model. Follow the manufacturer's instructions regarding periodic lubrication and other maintenance.

Detailing and running quality have both improved dramatically in the last 10 to 15 years. The wide availability of factory-installed DCC decoders and sound (and the many aftermarket decoders designed for specific models) has helped increase N scale's popularity.

Rolling stock

Most N scale cars are injection-molded styrene shells attached to a metal floor, metal frame, or plastic underframe with a weight hidden in the body. Detail on most models today is very good, as often exemplified by having separate running boards and ladders.

Passenger cars in N scale also have outstanding detail, with newer models featuring interior detail, **17**.

You'll find many older cars at swap meets, on eBay, and from other sources. Detail levels vary greatly, but this can

18

Atlas code 55 track (left) has a more accurate rail profile and better detail than Atlas code 80 (right), which has a grossly unrealistic rail height and cross section.

be an economical way to build up a freight car fleet, and improving older models' performance is often a simple matter of swapping out a car's old trucks for a new pair of Micro-Trains trucks with truck-mounted couplers.

(Chapter 6 goes into more details on locomotives and freight cars.)

Track

Until fairly recently, most N scale sectional and flextrack was code 80 (rails .080" tall). This is extremely heavy compared to prototype track, scaling out far larger than any track in real life. Smaller, more realistic track is now widely available, including Atlas, Micro Engineering, and Peco code 55 (the Peco track is actually code 80 rail,

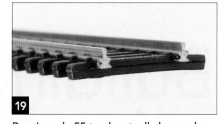

19

Peco's code 55 track actually has code 80 rail, but the lower .025" is imbedded in the tie strip. This results in strong track with a realistic profile.

with the bottom .025" sunk into the plastic tie strip), **18** and **19**.

I recommend starting with code 55 track right away. Its appearance is much more realistic than code 80, and the quality and durability of all brands is fine if handled with reasonable care. Early N scale locomotives and rolling stock had deep wheel flanges that wouldn't operate on lower-profile rail, but models today have smaller flanges, so this is no longer an issue.

Because N scale locomotives are significantly lighter than HO models, they are more affected by dirty and dusty trackwork, so you may find yourself cleaning the track more frequently. (See chapter 8 for more details on track.)

1

CHAPTER FIVE

Building models

These HO storefront structures started out as easy-to-build plastic structure kits from DPM (Woodland Scenics), Smalltown USA, City Classics, and Walthers. They were assembled, painted, and had signs and decals added. The vehicles are from Classic Metal Works, the figures from Preiser, and the streets are from Walthers.

There are more ready-to-run and assembled models available today than ever before, but that doesn't mean that model building is a lost art. You'll find many opportunities to assemble a structure kit, add details to a locomotive or freight car, and paint and weather a model.

This HO depot from GC Laser is an example of a laser-cut wood kit. Wood kits generally have more pieces than plastic kits, and they must be painted.

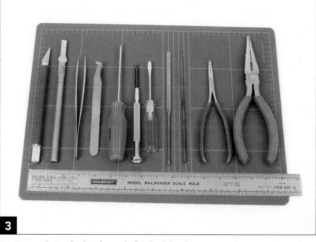

Basic tools include (from left): hobby knives with nos. 11 and 17 blades, tweezers, sprue nippers, small screwdrivers, needle files, needlenose pliers, and a scale rule. A self-healing cutting mat is also handy.

Many model railroaders consider model building to be the focal point of their hobby. For others, building models is just a prelude to getting trains running and operating. Either way, you'll benefit from mastering some basic modeling skills and learning about the tools, materials, and paints you will need.

Materials in kits and models

Model railroading has become largely a plastic hobby. The vast majority of models today are made of injection-molded styrene plastic, **1**. Most locomotives and freight cars have injection-molded styrene shells, with separately applied details of plastic or metal. Most structure kits are likewise injection-molded plastic.

Wood is also a common material. Many structure kits feature wood construction, with most today consisting of parts laser-cut from basswood or thin plywood sheet. Although these are more complex than plastic kits, they are buildable by most modelers who have put a few models together, **2**. The biggest challenge is that they require painting.

A craftsman kit is a subset of wood kits, which has many kit parts that must be cut to size, making it more challenging than a laser-cut kit.

As you get further into the hobby, you'll discover kits and details made of polyester resin. Resin is commonly used for limited-run, often highly detailed freight car and structure kits, as well as for small detail items. This material appears similar to plastic, but it must be glued with super glue or epoxy instead of plastic solvent.

Tools

You don't need an extensive tool kit right away, but you'll find there are several basic tools that you should have. Let's look at putting together a basic modeler's took kit, **3**.

The first tool on your list is a hobby knife. Although X-Acto has almost become synonymous with hobby knives, they are also available from Excel, Mascot, and others. Many styles of handles are available—just find one that fits your hand comfortably. A no. 11 blade (sharply angled with a fine point) works for most applications, but you'll also want to get some no. 17 blades that have a squared-off, chisel-shaped tip.

Blades become dull from frequent use, and the tip of a no. 11 blade is prone to break because of its fine point. When a blade becomes dull or chipped, discard it and use a fresh blade. By buying blades in bulk packs (50 or 100), you'll always have a new one available.

When discarding a blade, don't throw it in the trash. For safety, use a sharps disposal container (small ones are available from most large home supply stores or industrial tool suppliers).

A scale rule is vital for measuring models and plans. Scale rules have markings for one or more modeling scales on their edges, and steel or plastic ones are available in various lengths (6" and 12" are the most common). A steel rule also doubles as a straightedge guide when cutting materials with a hobby knife.

I consider tweezers and needlenose pliers vital as well. Tweezers with a fine, pointed tip are invaluable when handling small detail parts or when placing larger parts on a model. Needlenose pliers are heftier than tweezers, allowing you to get a firm grip on small parts, but they are smaller than standard pliers, so you can get into tight spaces.

If you build a lot of plastic models and kits, consider buying a fine-tip sprue cutter. Available from Micro-Mark and others, these tools cut parts from plastic sprues very cleanly.

Needle files and/or small sanding sticks will help you clean up imperfections on parts, including spots where they are cut from their sprues.

The screws typically used on freight cars and locomotives for mounting trucks and couplers require tools much smaller than common household versions. For these, you'll find a set of small screwdrivers with standard (slotted) and Phillips (cross pattern) heads handy.

4

Commonly used hobby adhesives include cyanoacrylate adhesive (super glue), liquid plastic cement, gel-type plastic cement, and clear parts adhesive.

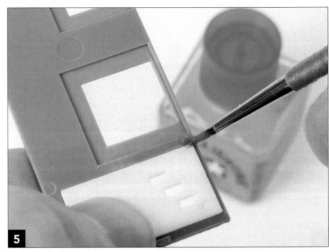

5

By touching a brush of liquid cement to mating pieces (always do this from the back), the cement will wick into the joint.

You'll also need a place to work on models, and you'll find you're more inclined to work on models if your space is warm, brightly lit, and inviting. A small workbench is ideal; a desk that you can devote to the purpose (even a small, inexpensive student desk) also works.

Some modelers manage to share their working space with family, perhaps in a living room or rec room, provided you can keep tools in a toolbox and have boxes where current

projects and parts can be stored. This approach can add to family time, and force you to work neatly and clean up after your projects.

Remember that your working surface will be subject to knife blades, glue drips, and possible paint spills. Keep it covered with a blade-friendly cover that can be easily replaced. You can simply use a large piece of cardboard, replacing it when it becomes cut and frayed. A better choice is a self-healing cutting mat, available in many sizes from X-Acto, Xuron, Excel, Mascot, and others. The rubberized surface of these mats help keep materials from sliding while being cut or worked on. They are firm, but allow the tip of a blade to go into the surface.

As you gain more experience, and begin to discover your favorite areas of the hobby, you'll find many other tools that you can use.

Glues

The number of adhesives currently on the market is staggering, but I find I can get 98 percent of my modeling done with four: liquid plastic cement (two types), super glue (also called cyanoacrylate adhesive or CA), clear parts adhesive, and white glue (or wood glue), **4**.

For almost any plastic-to-plastic joint, use liquid plastic cement. Liquid plastic cement isn't a glue, but a solvent that effectively melts each surface being bonded. When held together firmly,

the two plastic surfaces fuse to form an extremely strong joint.

There are two main types of plastic cement: liquid and gel. Liquid, such as Testor's Liquid Plastic Cement (no. 3502) and Tamiya Extra Thin Cement (no. 87038) is applied with a brush. Gel, such as Testor's Liquid Cement for Plastic Models (no. 3507) and Model Master (no. 8872), is applied with an applicator needle built into the container.

Use a liquid when you can hold or clamp a part or joint in place, such as a window frame in a wall, **5**. Touching a brush of liquid to the joint from the back will wick the liquid into the joint and create a tight bond. Many bottles have built-in brushes, but these are often too large for most uses. Instead, have a small paintbrush dedicated for glue. (I mark mine with a piece of blue tape on the handle, so it doesn't get mixed in with the brushes I use for paint.)

Use a gel in other instances by applying the glue to the joint, **6**, and then pressing the parts together and holding them for a few seconds until the gel has set (full curing requires longer), **7**. You'll develop a feel for which glue to use in different situations as you build models.

With either type of plastic cement, make sure you keep it off the model's surface: plastic cement will etch the surface and remove or mar paint. Also, make sure mating surfaces are free of

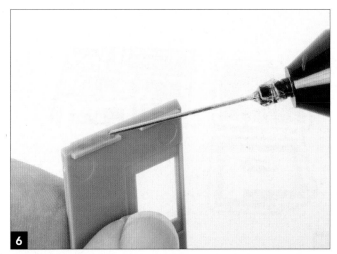

6

Gel-type plastic cement dispensers have needlepoint applicators. Carefully apply the cement to one surface to be joined.

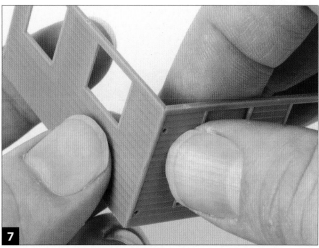

7

Press the joint together and hold it for several seconds until the cement takes hold. Then set the parts aside to dry.

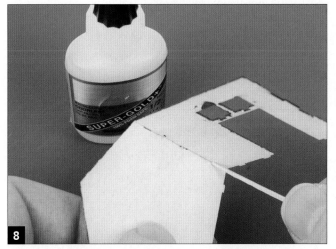

8

The best way to apply cyanoacrylate adhesive is often by placing a drop or two on a piece of cardstock and transferring it with a toothpick. This is a laser-cut wood kit wall joint.

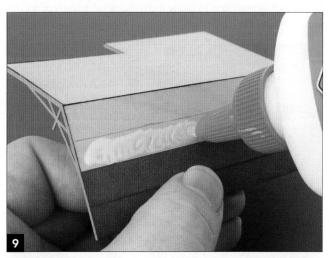

9

White glue works well for paper, wood, and cardstock. Here, a thin coat on a wood roof holds the strips of paper roofing (simulated tar paper).

paint. Because they work by solvent action, plastic cements will not work with non-plastics (resin, paper, metal) or when joining plastic to a different material.

Super glue is available in several viscosities from extra thin to thick. Thin CA bonds instantly but can be hard to control. Thick CA provides much more working time, and is gap-filling. My preference for most uses is medium—it provides a few seconds of time before setting hard, and it allows more control than thin CA when you apply it.

Use CA for bonding metal, resin, or dissimilar materials (plastic to brass, wood to plastic, etc.). It also works well for wood-to-wood joints or plastic-to-plastic when the mating area is small

and you need an instant bond. Super glue is best applied by placing a few drops on a scrap piece of cardstock or plastic, and then using a toothpick or pin to transfer it to the model, **8**.

Use white glue for porous materials such as wood, cardboard, mat board, and paper, **9**. Wood or yellow glue (aliphatic resin) is similar but provides a stronger, waterproof joint. A toothpick works well for applying it to small mating areas. These glues set slower than CA, so you'll need to keep joints firmly together for several minutes until the glue begins to set.

Clear parts cement, such as Testor's no. 3615, is the smart choice any time you're gluing clear styrene (such as structure windows or locomotive cab windows). It dries clear and glossy,

so if any happens to get on a window or other clear surface, it won't be noticeable. Don't use CA for clear parts—CA will cause them to fog. Also don't use regular plastic cement as it will mar a clear surface if any gets on it.

Modeling techniques

If it's been a while since you've put a model kit together—or if you've never done it before—start small. Kits range in complexity, even for similar models, as shown by the two HO freight car kits in photo **10**. A great place to start is a basic plastic structure kit, **11**. Take things step by step, and work slowly—regardless of the scale or size, building a model is simply a matter of repeatedly cutting and putting parts together.

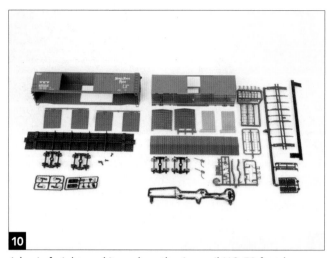

10

A basic freight car kit, such as the Accurail HO 50-foot boxcar at left, is a good model to start with. The Branchline (Atlas) 40-foot kit at the right includes many more (and finer) parts, including separate ends, ladders, grab irons, and the roof.

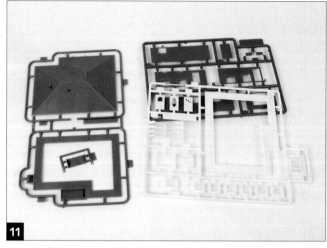

11

A typical injection-molded structure kit, such as this HO Walthers ranch house, has a roof, walls, window frames, and other parts attached to various colored sprues.

12

Remove parts from sprues with a hobby knife or sprue cutter (shown here).

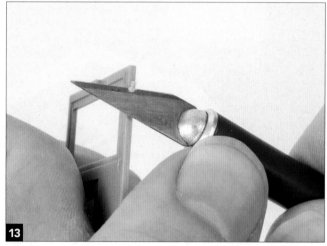

13

Carefully trim flash or stray sprue material from parts with a hobby knife.

Start by pulling out all the parts and identifying them against the instructions. Most instructions include an exploded view of the model (some simple kits have only an illustration). Plastic parts are usually attached to a sprue, and in larger kits, the sprue might have an identification number next to the part. Don't remove these numbered parts until you need one.

Cut parts from sprues with a hobby knife or sprue cutter, **12**. **Never** twist or pull parts from sprues—it will likely leave a divot or scar on the part that can't be hidden. Use the edge of a knife blade, a needle file, or sanding stick to clean any extra material from the sprue that's left on the part, **13** and **14**. Use a hobby knife to trim any flash (stray

material from the molding process that sometimes remains on a part).

Test-fit all joints before adding glue. On larger kits, many parts often look similar. Always double-check to make sure you have the correct part and use the appropriate glue.

Build kits in subassemblies, letting the glue dry in one area while working on another. When gluing together structure walls, let each corner dry completely before moving to the next one.

Paint smaller parts prior to adding them to main assemblies. For example, if you want to paint window frames a different color, do it before gluing them to the walls and adding the clear glazing.

Paint

The amount of painting you have to do depends upon the type of models you acquire or build, the level of realism and detail you're trying to achieve, and the level of weathering that you wish to do. Plastic structures can almost always use a coat of paint to kill the plastic shine, even if they're "molded in realistic colors" (as manufacturers say).

You'll find it handy to have several colors of model paints, along with a variety of brushes. Many modelers eventually acquire airbrushes; for now, you can use spray cans if needed.

I recommend using water-based (acrylic) model paints. Today's acrylic paints are a far cry from the first acrylics of the 1960s and 1970s, when most

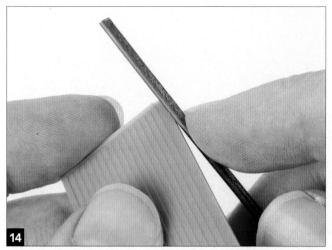

A needle file or fine sanding stick works well for smoothing edges.

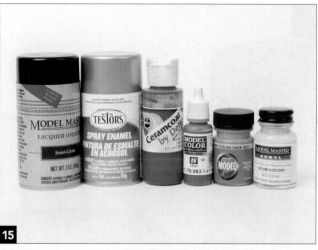

Popular paint for models includes spray paints (Model Master and Testors), craft paint (Ceramcoat), and bottles of model paint (Vallejo, Modelflex, and Model Master Acryl).

You'll find several sizes of brushes useful, including wide and narrow flat brushes for painting large surfaces and round brushes down to 0 and 5/0 for detail work.

Apply paint evenly across the surface. When applying successive brushfuls of paint, brush back toward the previously applied (still wet) paint—this avoids marks created from paint drying in different areas.

model paints were organic-solvent-based. Acrylics cover well, adhere to almost any surface, and are easy to use. They are also safe (no solvent vapors) and clean up with water.

Brands include Badger Modelflex, Model Master Acryl, Micro-Mark MicroLux, and Vallejo, **15**. A tremendous variety of colors is available, including standard colors and those that match specific railroad paint schemes. You'll also find weathering colors like grimy black (dark gray), mud, and dust and rust colors such as rust, roof brown, rail brown, and railroad tie brown.

The enemy of acrylic paint is air. Leaving a bottle open for even a few minutes will dry the paint around the lip of the bottle and along the inner sides. When painting, it's best to use an eyedropper or pipette to transfer the paint into a small aluminum artist's palette or other surface so you can keep the bottle closed.

Once acrylic paint dries, it will not reflow. So if you have a bottle where skin has formed under the lid or edges, carefully remove the skin with tweezers or a toothpick. Also, keep the threads and lips on paint bottles and caps wiped clean of paint. If small flecks of dried paint fall into the paint, you may accidentally brush them onto the surface of a model, leading to frustration.

A few brushes will serve your initial needs. Buy good quality brushes, but they don't have to be top-quality artist's design, **16**. Standard round brushes are sized by number: the smaller the number, the smaller the brush. Flat brushes are sized by dimension. Get a few standard brushes: nos. 0, 1, 2, and 3, and a few flat brushes from ¼" to ½" and you'll be set. Synthetic brushes are good all-around brushes for modeling.

Wet the brush with water prior to painting (this helps keep paint from drying immediately upon contact with dry bristles, which makes cleanup easier). Dip the ends of the bristles in the paint. Brush the surface in the same direction as any features such as siding, **17**. Use

18

Westco is an example of a scratchbuilt building. Gerry Leone built the HO structure using wood siding, window castings, stripwood, and other detail items. *Gerry Leone*

as few strokes as possible—let the paint level itself to avoid brush marks.

You can use single coats if you're painting a color similar to the surface; other colors, especially lighter ones, may require two or three coats. Let each coat dry to the touch before applying a following coat. With acrylics, you can use a hair dryer to speed up drying time.

Clean you brushes under running water, adding a drop of dish detergent and working it into the bristles. Rinse the brush until all traces of paint are gone, dry it, and store it bristles-up in an open container.

Never leave brushes sitting in thinner, and don't jab brushes into a bottle of thinner to clean them—both practices will damage the bristles and change the shape of the brush.

Scratchbuilding

You'll hear the term *scratchbuilding* regarding building models. The term means to build a model from raw components—from scratch—using sheet and strip styrene, textured (simulated) brick and wood sheets, and other details, **18**. It's most common with structures, although some accomplished modelers scratchbuild rolling stock and even locomotives. It's beyond the scope of this book, but something to explore, if interested, as you gain experience.

Another term you'll hear is *kitbashing*. This has become the popular term for taking one or more kits and modifying them by combining components to create a new building, or taking two or three identical kits and combining them to make a larger version. It's

another modeling technique to try as you improve your skills.

Dive in!

The best way to gain experience is to simply pick up a kit and start working on it. Your skills will improve as you do more modeling, and you'll learn techniques through experience. There are many books out there that go into great detail on building models (many of which are listed on page 36).

I highly recommend subscribing to one of the monthly model railroading magazines. They're full of great modeling ideas, tips, and techniques, as well as providing information on new materials and kits. Having that monthly dose of inspiration is often just the ticket for getting back to the workbench to embark on a new project.

1

CHAPTER SIX

Locomotives and freight cars

Locomotives and rolling stock (freight and passenger cars) are the heart of any model railroad. Locomotive and car models are available representing prototypes of all eras, including steam locomotives, early and modern diesels, and early wood freight cars through today's jumbo covered hoppers and tank cars, **1**.

Broadway Limited's beautiful HO model of a Pennsylvania Railroad K4s Pacific (4-6-2) steam locomotive includes much detail, including piping, cab interior and figures, handrails, grab irons, number plate, builder's plate, and many separate detail items. It also includes a Digital Command Control (DCC) sound decoder with speaker and a smoke unit.

2

3

There's not much empty space inside a typical diesel model. This WalthersProto HO GP20 chassis includes a SoundTraxx DCC decoder on the circuit board. The motor and flywheel are visible, with a cast-metal weight surrounding it. *Bill Zuback*

This N scale Atlas SD60 chassis shows typical features, including a five-pole, skew-wound motor, two flywheels, a circuit-board DCC decoder, and a cast-metal split frame. *Bill Zuback*

4

5

The Atlas N scale Baldwin VO1000 switcher represents a prototype built from 1939 through the mid-1940s. Baldwin was a minority builder, but its locomotives are popular with modelers.

The EMD F7 is a successor to the pioneering FT diesel. The F7 was the most common cab diesel built: 3,700 from 1948–1953. This HO Rock Island model is from Athearn's Genesis line.

Let's start with a look at diesel locomotives and then steam locomotives and rolling stock. We'll look at what makes a good model and trace how prototype equipment evolved through the years using models as examples.

Diesel models

As the chapters on modeling scales explained, today's models are better than ever before, with exquisite details (often matching specific prototypes) and superb running characteristics, and many come factory equipped with Digital Command Control (DCC) decoders and sound units.

Exact construction varies among manufacturers and scales, but most follow the same basic layout of components. A plastic shell rests atop a metal frame, which holds the motor and mechanism, **2**.

Scale models are powered by small DC motors. Most newer models feature an enclosed or can design; others are open, with skew-wound, five-pole motors. Drive shafts extend out of both ends of the motor to drive the forward and rear trucks.

Most models have a flywheel attached to the drive shaft, although

some have two, one on each end of the motor. Often made of brass, these heavy pieces help smooth operation by keeping the drive shaft turning even if power is briefly lost, **3**.

Universal joints and a series of gears transfer motion from the drive shaft downward through the truck tower to gears on each axle. These components are made of engineering plastic.

Metal wheels are mounted on insulated axles, and the wheels on each rail pick up electricity. Wipers and wires carry power to a circuit board atop the frame. This circuit board holds electrical components, including diodes for lighting (and sometimes the bulbs or LEDs themselves) and circuitry for a DCC decoder or a socket for a decoder that can be installed later (more on that in chapter 9).

There's not a lot of basic maintenance to be done on modern locomotive models. It's best to not even remove the shell if you don't have to. Follow the manufacturer's instructions on lubrication, using a drop or two of plastic-compatible light oil (such as LaBelle no. 108) on a truck gear if needed. If you use too

much, overlubrication attracts dirt and dust, which defeats the purpose of lubrication in the first place.

The most important feature of a locomotive is smooth operation—if it doesn't run well, you'll be frustrated no matter how nice it looks. Models should run quietly at all speeds, with no grinding or excess motor noise, start smoothly, without jerking into motion, and run smoothly at very low speeds as well as high speeds.

Models should be well proportioned and accurately match their prototypes. The paint and lettering should be accurate for the railroads they represent. Paint separation lines should be neat and clean, and lettering should be legible (not smudged or blurry).

Most model locomotives today fit the bill. You might also come across used locomotives, or new-in-box locomotives that were produced many years ago. This can be a very economical way to build a locomotive fleet, as many very good models were built in the 1990s and even earlier. These include Athearn and Atlas standard lines, Kato, Proto 2000, Stewart, and InterMountain.

6

This is Kato's N scale model of an EMD E8 passenger diesel. They were built from 1948–1953, and some remained in service for Amtrak and commuter agencies through the 1980s.

7

Electro-Motive's GP7 made the hood-unit diesel popular, as more than 2,700 were built from 1949–1954. This is an HO model wearing Burlington's 1950s scheme from WalthersProto.

8

Low noses became an option in the late 1950s. EMD's GP20, built from 1959–1962, was the builder's first turbocharged diesel. This is an HO WalthersProto model. *Bill Zuback*

9

The Alco RS-2, built from 1945–1950, was the 1,500-hp successor to the pioneering RS-1. This is an HO model in Green Bay & Western colors from Walthers Proto 1000.

A key consideration is that most locomotives into the 1990s—even top-end models—were not built with DCC in mind. Most don't have prewired sockets for decoders, so decoders have to be hard-wired, which can be difficult on many models (especially in N scale).

When examining older models, look for all wheels powered and all-wheel electrical pickup. Check the level of body detail. In general, a lower quality model will have more details cast in place and fewer separate details—and the heavier and less realistic those details will be. Check the detail in rooftop fans, door latches and hinges, grills, and screens.

Prototype diesels

Knowing what diesel models are appropriate for which eras can be tricky, but having a basic understanding will help you make better buying decisions. Diesels began appearing in significant numbers in the 1930s, with switching locomotives from Alco, Electro-Motive Corp., and then Baldwin, along with high-speed passenger locomotives from Electro-Motive and Alco, **4**. The diesel engine initially proved its worth in those

seemingly opposite situations: slow-moving engines in which lots of tractive effort, but not much speed, was needed, and high-speed, lightweight trains where high tractive effort wasn't needed.

The challenge came in mainline freight service, where locomotives require both high tractive effort to get heavy trains started and high horsepower to get them moving at high speeds. Mainline steam locomotives of the late 1930s were very powerful machines, with many rated at 5,000 or more horsepower.

The first successful road freight diesel was EMC's streamlined FT, introduced in 1939. Although each locomotive was just 1,350 horsepower, several could be coupled together and connected electrically under control of one engineer. Thus, the four-unit demonstrator set (in A-B-B-A configuration, with the middle two locomotives cabless) was 5,400 horsepower, which rivaled big steam locomotives.

Diesels proved less expensive to maintain, required fewer fuel stops, and needed no water stops—a major factor for railroads in desert and arid areas. Railroads went for diesels in a big way.

Electro-Motive (Electro-Motive Division, or EMD after 1941) dominated the early market with its series of cab unit streamlined four-axle freight F units (FT, followed by F2, F3, F7, and F9) and six-axle passenger E units (EA and E1 through E9 through the 1950s, **5** and **6**. EMD's main rival was former steam builder Alco, which offered a streamlined freight diesel (FA) and a passenger diesel (PA).

The cab unit style was attractive, but it didn't allow easy access to the engine and other components, and it made switching moves difficult because of poor rear visibility. The answer was the road switcher, or hood unit, which was identified by short and long narrow hoods on either side of the cab and walkways along the hoods.

Alco's RS-1 of 1941 is credited as the first hood unit, but it was EMD's 1,500-hp GP7 of 1949 that spurred the style's popularity, **7**. EMD continued to dominate the market, with GP (four-axle) and SD (six-axle) designs becoming bigger and more powerful. The 1960s saw the 2,000-hp GP20, the 3,000-hp GP40 and SD40, and the 3,600-hp SD45, **8**.

10

Alco's 1960s Century line wasn't enough to save the company. This is the four-axle, 2,400-hp C-424. This HO Canadian National model is from Atlas, part of its Classic Gold line.

11

EMD's GP38-2 was its most popular late-model four-axle diesel, with more than 2,200 sold from 1972–1987. This is an HO model from Walthers Proto 2000.

12

The SD60 was front-line power in the 1980s, as EMD built 537 of the six-axle, 3,800-hp engines from 1984–1991. This is an N scale model from Atlas in Oakway Leasing colors. *Bill Zuback*

13

EMD's F40PH passenger diesel was very successful, with various versions in production from 1976–1992. This HO scale F40PH-2D from Rapido wears VIA Rail's Canada scheme.

Alco kept pace with succeeding RS models (and six-axle RSDs) and then introduced its Century line around 1960, producing the four-axle C-420 (2,000 hp) and C-424 (2,400 hp) and the six-axle C-628 (2,800 hp), C-630 (3,000 hp), and C-636 (3,600 hp) before exiting the locomotive market in 1969, **9** and **10**.

In the 1960s, GE entered the road diesel market with its Universal line, starting with the U25B (four-axle) and U25C (six-axle; middle numbers indicate horsepower in hundreds), followed by the U28, U30, U33, and U36 models into the 1970s (see sidebar on page 22).

EMD continued with its Dash-2 line from the 1970s into the '80s, which were upgraded versions of earlier diesels, and then moved to its SD50, SD60, SD70, SD75, SD80, and SD90 models from the 1990s into the 2000s, with horsepower moving to 4,000 and then 4,400 hp (with a brief effort at 6,000-plus hp), **11** and **12**. EMD also produced the popular 3,000-hp F40PH line of four-axle passenger diesels, **13**.

During that period, GE brought out first its Dash-7 line, then the Dash-8 and Dash-9 line of 3,000 to 4,400-hp locomotives, followed by the 4,400-hp AC4400CW. GE also offered the P40 and P42 passenger engines, **14**.

Today, GE dominates locomotive production, making versions of its six-axle ES44 (4,400 hp), while EMD offers its SD70ACe (see photo 3 on page 29), **15**.

Trends included a shift to six-axle diesels for freight service in the 1960s, with freight engines exclusively six-axle by the 1990s, and a move to AC traction motors for heavy-haul service by the mid-1990s. Both builders offer AC and DC versions of their current models.

Prototype locomotives often varied in appearance through their production runs (some were in production 10 or more years). In addition, each prototype railroad tended to prefer different features or options, such as the type of horns, headlights, brakes, and bell. This was especially true through the 1960s, when 100-plus railroads were ordering locomotives.

You'll find entire books dedicated to individual locomotive models, manufacturers, locomotive series, and locomotive rosters of individual railroads. Don't overlook early builders, such as Baldwin, Lima, and Fairbanks-Morse, all of which produced comparatively few locomotives. All were out of the locomotive business by the mid-1950s, but they remain popular among railfans and modelers.

Steam models

Steam locomotives have always been popular with modelers, and rightly so—they are fascinating machines with many moving parts on display. The design of model steam locomotives leaves less space inside the boiler than does a comparable diesel, meaning manufacturers have to cram more things into a tight space. Many models use the tender for electronic gear, such as a decoder and speaker (as shown in photo 16 on page 33), and use tender wheels for electrical pickup. This means many steam models have a plug-and-socket connection between the locomotive and tender.

14

General Electric's P42 4,250-hp passenger diesels, built from 1995–2001, can still be found leading Amtrak trains across the country. This is an HO model from Kato.

15

General Electric's 4,400-hp ES44AC, or GEVO (GE Evolution Series) diesel, debuted in 2005 and remains in production. This HO model is from MTH.

16

The 2-6-0 Mogul, although bumped from mainline service just after 1900, remained a popular branchline engine through the end of the steam era. This is an N scale model from Bachmann.

17

The USRA version of the 4-8-2 Light Mountain steam locomotive was operated by several railroads. This N scale version is a Bachmann Spectrum model.

Historically, it's always been more of a challenge to get steam locomotives to operate as smoothly as diesels. This is a function of the complex mechanism (as with the real thing) involving side rods and valve gear, and finding a good way to couple the drive shaft with the drivers.

Today's steam locomotive models feature outstanding details and much better operation compared to older models. Many newer offerings are based on specific prototype locomotives and include details to match specific versions or eras. More details are separate, including bells, whistles, pumps, and piping, and most models have detailed cabs that feature figures and backhead detail. Valve gear and rods are more accurately represented, and rods are typically blackened metal (many older models have shiny stamped metal pieces).

The biggest improvement is that steam models are now available with DCC and sound. Adding DCC to older steam locomotives is certainly possible, but it can be very

Common steam locomotive types

Whyte Class	Name	Service	Primary era
0-6-0	Switcher	Yard service	1800s to early 1900s
0-8-0	Switcher	Yard service	1900s to 1950s
2-6-0	Mogul	Freight	late 1800s to early 1900s
2-6-2	Prairie	Freight	late 1800s to early 1900s
2-8-0	Consolidation	Freight	1900 to mid-1900s
2-8-2	Mikado	Freight	early 1900s to end of steam era
2-8-4	Berkshire	Freight	1920s to 1950s
2-10-0	Decapod	Freight	1920s to 1950s
2-10-2	Santa Fe	Freight	1920s to 1930s
4-4-0	American	Freight and passenger	mid- to late 1800s
4-4-2	Atlantic	Passenger	late 1800s to early 1900s
4-6-0	Ten-Wheeler	Freight and passenger	late 1800s to early 1900s
4-6-2	Pacific	Passenger	early to mid-1900s
4-6-4	Hudson	Passenger	late 1920s to 1940s
4-8-2	Mountain	Freight	early 1900s to 1950s
4-8-4	Northern*	Freight and passenger	1920s to 1950s
2-6-6-2	Mallet	Freight	early 1900s to 1950s
2-8-8-2	Mallet	Freight	1910s to 1950s
4-6-6-4	Challenger	Freight and passenger	1930s to 1950s
4-8-8-4	Big Boy	Freight	1940s to 1950s

*Also known as Dixies on several Southern railroads

The 4-8-4 Northern became the most common "modern" fast freight and passenger locomotive at the end of the steam era. This Kato N scale model matches Union Pacific's FEF-3 class, one of which, no. 844, still serves the UP.

The USRA light 2-10-2 (known as a Santa Fe) wasn't as common as other locomotive types, but it was still operated by six railroads. This is an HO Bachmann Spectrum model.

The USRA standard 2-8-8-2, based on a Norfolk & Western design, was a low-speed, powerful freight locomotive. This HO model is from Walthers' Proto 2000 Heritage series.

challenging, even for experienced modelers.

When looking at older models, test-run them if possible. Many older models run well, but some don't—and trying to troubleshoot the binding, jerking motion and poor slow-speed operation of many older steam models is not an easy task.

For maintenance, a drop or two of oil on drive gears periodically is often all it takes. This is usually done via a removable cover under the drivers, but check instruction manuals for specific directions. Otherwise, don't remove a boiler shell if you can avoid it.

Prototype steam locomotives

Steam locomotives grew in size from the 1800s through the end of the steam era in the 1940s and 1950s. With steam locomotives, each railroad had its own design, with locomotives from each railroad having a distinctive appearance. An exception was a series of designs developed by the United States Railroad Administration

(USRA) from the period of USRA control of U.S. railroads during, and immediately after, World War I.

Steam locomotives are classified by wheel arrangement (called the *Whyte system*), which lists the number of lead, driving, and trailing wheels. The chart on page 45 shows common wheel arrangements and their names, along with their most popular periods of operation.

The drivers, or driving wheels, are the large wheels connected by rods. They provide the power for moving the locomotive. Locomotives in mainline service have two- or four-wheel trucks at the front. These lead, or pilot, trucks help balance the weight of the locomotive and help guide and stabilize it around curves. The trailing, or rear, trucks found on many locomotives help support the weight of the firebox and ensure smooth operation in reverse.

Many locomotive types are also known by nicknames for their wheel arrangements. For example,

a locomotive with two pilot wheels, eight drivers (four on each side), and two trailing wheels, is a 2-8-2. This arrangement is known as a Mikado.

Some locomotives remained in service for a long time. For example, 2-6-0 Moguls became too small for increasing mainline train sizes by World War I, but their light weight made them ideal for branch lines, and many remained in service through the end of the steam era, **16**.

Popular freight locomotives during the key modeling eras of the 1920s to the 1950s were the Mikado and later the 2-8-4 Berkshire, 4-8-2 Mountain, and 4-8-4 Northern, **17** and **18**. The most common passenger locomotives were the 4-6-2 Pacific, the 4-6-4 Hudson, and Northerns. Other wheel arrangements were less common, such as the 2-10-0 and 2-10-2, **19**.

Articulated steam locomotives of various types were common in both mountainous territory as low-speed pullers and—from the late 1930s—on level ground as fast

21

The USRA 0-6-0 switcher, represented here by an HO Walthers Proto 2000 Heritage model, was superseded in popularity by the 0-8-0 in the 1920s and later.

22

This N scale Micro-Trains car represents a USRA design 40-foot, single-sheathed (wood planks on exterior steel braces) boxcar, common from the 1920s to the 1950s.

23

The Milwaukee Road built boxcars to its own welded design, with distinctive horizontal side ribs. This HO model of a 40-foot version is from InterMountain.

24

Insulated boxcars began to appear in the late 1950s. This plug-door, 50-foot HO model from Moloco represents a 1960s prototype.

runners. Articulateds are essentially two locomotives under a single boiler, with both sets of drivers listed, such as 2-8-8-2, **20**. Probably the best-known articulateds were Union Pacific's successful 4-8-8-4 Big Boys, built in the late 1930s and early 1940s and recognized as the largest steam locomotives built.

Switchers lacked lead and trailing trucks, and had smaller drivers than road locomotives. The 0-6-0 was common through the early 1900s, with the more powerful 0-8-0 built in higher numbers after World War II, **21**. Both could be found in service through the end of steam.

Diesels began taking over for steam in large numbers in the 1940s. Dieselization was rapid; by the mid-1950s, steam locomotives had largely vanished from American railroads.

A challenge for model manufacturers has long been that, unlike prototype diesels—where the same model was sold en masse to dozens or hundreds of railroads—steam locomotives were, with few exceptions, customized for each railroad. This

means, for example, that Broadway Limited's beautiful HO Pennsylvania K4s Pacific can't accurately represent a 4-6-2 from any other railroad, **1**. In spite of this—and good for modelers— manufacturers continue to offer new models, even if their potential markets are limited.

Rolling stock models

Twenty years ago, to get a beautifully detailed, prototypically accurate freight car with knuckle couplers and metal wheelsets, you had to build a complex kit, add aftermarket details to it, and possibly paint it and add decals. Today, you can simply open a box.

This quality comes with a significant price tag as well. It can be difficult to assemble a large fleet of rolling stock without breaking the bank. The good news is that more economical models are also available. You can still find kits (especially in HO), and older kits and cars can still be found at swap meets, from eBay, and through other sources. Many of these are still good models, and they can be upgraded as you gain experience.

Avoid older train-set quality cars of the AHM/Tyco type. These typically had out-of-scale, clunky details, bad paint schemes, poor quality trucks and wheels, and truck-mounted horn-hook couplers.

Prototype freight cars

It's easy to start buying freight cars at random, based simply on appealing or favorite road names and paint schemes, and ending up with a collection that doesn't make sense in terms of era being modeled or prototype use.

Cars have evolved significantly since the steam era. Gone are the days when the 40-foot boxcar hauled everything from canned goods to bulk corn. Modern cars are larger in length and have increased the weight of the load they carry. They have become specialized, with many being designed and equipped to carry specific products.

At the turn of the 20th century, a typical car had a wood body and wood frame, was about 30 feet long, and had a capacity of 20 to 40 tons. By the 1920s, freight cars with steel frames, and having

25

Excess-height boxcars appeared in the 1960s, usually equipped for auto parts or other specialized service. This 60-foot, double-plug-door, 1970s-era N scale car is from Micro-Trains.

26

There are still 50-foot general-service boxcars out there, many dating to the 1970s and '80s. This HO model of a SIECO-built Bay Colony car is from the Athearn Genesis series.

27

This two-bay, 55-ton offset-side hopper car is typical of those built from the 1930s through the 1950s. It's an N scale model from Micro-Trains.

28

Most modern coal unit trains now use large "bathtub" gondolas like this Bethgon Coalporter, with 100- to 110-ton capacity. DeLuxe Innovations makes this N scale model.

wood or steel bodies, became the norm. Capacity increased to 40 to 50 tons.

All-steel cars became common by the 1940s, with 70-ton cars coming into wide use by the late 1950s, and then 100-ton cars in the 1960s. Today, most modern cars have capacities of 100 to 110 tons.

The lifespan of a car depends on its type and service, but 25 to 30 years isn't unusual, and up to 40 years is possible without rebuilding. This means if you model 1980, you can get away with having a few 1950s-era cars in paint schemes for railroads that had been gone for several years.

Let's take a look at the various car types, see how they've evolved over the years, and review what each car type is used for.

Boxcars

By World War I, most boxcars were built with wood bodies atop steel underframes, and by the 1930s, steel construction was common. The 40-foot boxcar became common by 1920, with 40- and later 50-ton capacities, **22**. The 40-foot steel boxcar would remain the

most common car on railroads into the 1960s (photo 4 on page 23). Details varied by builder and design, with many types of roofs, ends, and doors being produced, **23**.

Boxcars were used to haul almost any type of cargo that would fit through the doors, including boxed and cased goods, automobiles (usually in 50-foot boxcars), and bulk products. Into the 1960s, boxcars were the standard car for carrying grain, with temporary doors tacked across the openings for loading.

By the late 1950s, 50-foot cars became more common, **24**. Cars with plug doors that sealed tighter protected canned and dry goods better, and insulated boxcars began carrying many products once carried by refrigerator cars.

The 1960s saw the birth of excess-height (*high-cube*) boxcars. Short cars were used in appliance service, while long (60- and 86-foot) cars were fitted with special racks for carrying auto parts, a high-priority service for railroads, **25**. The number of boxcars in service continued to decline.

Today, there are still general-purpose 50-foot cars in service, **26**, but most boxcars are specially equipped. Boxcars currently make up just 7 percent of the total freight car fleet, with about 111,000 in service.

Hoppers and gondolas

Hopper cars are open-top cars so named because bulk commodities can be unloaded via hoppers with doors at the bottom of the car. They are usually defined by their capacity in tons and/or the number of outlet bays they have. Hopper cars became virtually synonymous with coal cars, as that was their most common load. They are also used for carrying crushed limestone, ballast, rock, and other aggregate.

Hoppers were among the earliest all-steel cars (by the 1900s). By the 1920s, hoppers were typically two-bay cars of 50- to 55-ton capacity, **27**. Larger cars, with three or four bays and capacities of 50 to 70 tons, began appearing in the 1930s, and increased in popularity from the 1950s through the 1970s, with 100-ton cars appearing in the 1960s.

29

This N scale Micro-Trains model follows a prototype two-bay, 100-ton ACF Center-Flow covered hopper built for cement service from the 1970s onward.

30

Among the most common grain cars from the 1970s to the 2000s is the Pullman-Standard 4,750-cubic-foot, three-bay, 100-ton covered hopper. This HO version is from Tangent Scale Models.

31

The Trinity 5,161-cf, three-bay, 110-ton covered hopper has been in production since 1995. Athearn Genesis makes this HO scale version.

32

Pacific Fruit Express had the country's largest fleet of reefers, and its 40-foot class R-40-10 car was typical of steel ice cars built in the late 1930s and later. The HO model is from InterMountain.

Since the 1980s, much coal traffic shifted to large gondola cars—often called *bathtub gondolas*—as a majority of power plants and industrial customers use rotary unloaders to dump cars. Many are aluminum (the most common type of aluminum car) to save on weight and increase the payload, **28**.

Gondolas have also increased in size through the 1900s. Gons fall into two basic categories: mill and general service. Mill gons are typically longer cars with lower sides that are often used for finished products (and incoming scrap) of steel mills. Many have ends that fold down (*drop ends*) to allow for carrying longer loads.

General-service gons are typically not as long but have taller sides and ends. Their ends are fixed, but many have doors in the floor to allow dumping loads (*drop bottoms*). They commonly carried coal, aggregates, machinery, and bulky items.

Currently, hopper cars account for 9 percent of all cars in service (142,000), and gondolas are at 15 percent with 228,000 cars.

Covered hoppers

Covered hoppers make up almost a third of all freight cars in service today. They're the most common type of car (493,000), but they are a relatively new car type. They're labeled by their cubic capacity in feet and number of outlet bays, **29**.

The first covered hoppers were small 2,000-cubic foot (cf), two-bay cars, introduced in the 1930s for hauling bulk dry cement, sand, and lime—dense, heavy products. In the 1950s, covered hoppers grew, with 2,900-cf, three-bay cars carrying other products such as fertilizer, potash, and dry chemicals.

In the 1960s, regulatory rate changes made carrying corn and other bulk grains in covered hoppers a practical option. By the end of the 1970s, covered hoppers carried most of the grain traffic (prior to that, grain was bulk-loaded in boxcars). The most popular grain hoppers from the late 1960s into the 1980s were 4,650- and 4,750-cf cars, **30**, while today, 5,100- to 5,400-cf cars are common, **31**.

Covered hoppers also haul plastic pellets, sugar, flour, and almost any other powdered or granular commodity. Plastic pellets are carried in the largest covered hoppers, cars 60 feet or longer with capacities from 5,700 cf to over 6,000 cf.

Refrigerator cars

From the steam era through the 1960s, perishables such as fruits, vegetables, and meat were carried in ice-bunker refrigerator cars, known as *reefers*. These cars relied on ice, carried in end-of-car compartments (*bunkers*), to keep loads cool. Cars grew in size from 32 feet in the early 20th century to 36 and 40 feet in the 1920s and 1930s, and they went from wood body construction to steel in the late 1930s, **32**.

You can spot an ice-bunker car by the roof hatches (two at each end) used to load the ice. Most reefers had pairs of swinging doors on each side (compared to a boxcar's sliding doors), and in the 1950s, sliding plug doors became more common.

Cars cooled by mechanical refrigeration didn't become common

33

This BNSF/Western Fruit Express mechanical refrigerator car, a rebuilt version of a 1970s car, includes a DCC sound decoder and speaker. The HO model is from Athearn Genesis.

34

The newest mechanical reefers in service are these 64-foot, excess-height cars, built by Trinity beginning in 2003. This HO version is from BLMA Models.

35

Steam-era tank cars had a separate steel frame. This Atlas HO model represents a 1940s–1960s-era, 11,000-gallon pressurized car in propane service.

36

Modern LPG cars are the biggest tank cars in service. This Athearn Genesis HO model is a modern 33,900-gallon, frameless tank car.

until the 1960s. These cars were bigger than ice cars—50 feet and longer—and can be spotted by the grill or screen on the side at one end that covers a small engine and refrigeration equipment. By 1970, most ice cars were out of service.

Through the ice-bunker era, refrigerator cars were among the most colorful cars. Many reefers were yellow, orange, and bright red, standing out in a sea of brown and boxcar-red cars. Private owners (meat packers such as Swift and Wilson owned and leased large fleets) and companies controlled by railroads or groups of railroads, such as Pacific Fruit Express (held jointly by Southern Pacific and Union Pacific) owned most reefers.

After flirting with jumbo cryogenic cars (cooled by dry ice) in the 1990s, most reefers in service are mechanical cars in frozen-food service, **33** and **34**. Reefers today make up less than 1 percent of all cars (about 13,000 total).

Tank cars

Tank cars are currently the second-most common type of car, with about 371,000

(24 percent of all freight cars) in service. As with other cars, tank cars gradually increased in size, with 8,000- and 10,000-gallon cars common by the end of the steam era, and then 14,000- to 20,000-gallon cars by 1960, **35**. With the advent of 100-ton cars in the 1960s, tank cars kept growing, but late-1960s regulations capped tank car size at 33,900 gallons.

A major design change came in the late 1950s, when designers did away with a separate frame, instead relying on the tank itself for structural strength. Large expansion domes also disappeared and were replaced with smaller housing covering a manway and outlet controls.

Tank car size and design varies greatly by the commodity being carried. Most tanks carry petroleum and chemical products (refined fuel, crude oil, ethanol, LPG, ammonia, chlorine, molten sulfur, and various acids). Other common cargo includes corn syrup, vegetable oil, and kaolin clay slurry.

The denser a product, the smaller the car used. For example, corn syrup

(11.5 pounds per gallon) cars are relatively small, at about 13,000 gallons. Liquified Petroleum Gas (LPG) weighs just 4.6 pounds per gallon, which means modern LPG cars are the biggest tank cars in service, with capacities around 33,000 gallons, **36**.

Some tank cars are high-pressure cars, designed for carrying products such as anhydrous ammonia, chlorine, and LPG, which must be kept under pressure to keep them in liquid state.

Piggyback and container cars

A highway trailer riding on a railroad flatcar is known as a *piggyback*, or TOFC (trailer on flatcar), and a container is a COFC (container on flatcar), **37**. Together, TOFC and COFC constitute intermodal traffic.

A few railroads experimented with piggyback traffic in the 1930s and '40s, but it wasn't until the 1950s that TOFC began to grow, spurred by the formation of Trailer Train Co. (later TTX) in 1955. Owned by several railroads, TTX provided a pool of piggyback flatcars to member railroads, encouraging interchange

Long (89-foot) piggyback flats became common in the 1960s. This is a Walthers HO flatcar with an A-Line 40-foot trailer in a 1970s Chicago & North Western scheme.

Double-stack well cars are now the most common way to haul containers. This HO model of a Thrall five-unit articulated car is from A-Line, with 20-, 40-, and 45-foot containers.

traffic and increasing lengths of hauls. By the mid-1960s many railroads were operating significant TOFC traffic, including dedicated priority trains.

Into the 1950s, flatcars in TOFC service were old general-service cars converted to haul trailers. Delivered in 1955, the first cars designed specifically for piggyback service were 75-footers that could carry a pair of 35-foot trailers. By the late 1950s, 85-foot piggyback cars began appearing, and by the early 1960s, the 89-foot car was standard.

Trailers from the 1930s into the 1950s were typically 32 to 35 feet long,

and in 1957, the 40-foot trailer became legal across the country. That size remained standard (other than 28-foot "pup" trailers) until 1981, when the 45-foot trailer became legal. Additional size increases came in 1985 (48 feet) and 1991 (53 feet).

Rail container traffic began in the 1950s. The adaptation of international standards (ISO) for container sizes in 1965 spurred traffic growth, with 40- and 20-foot containers becoming the most common. Containers were typically carried on 89-foot flatcars until the development of the double-stack well car in the early 1980s, **38**. These cars have increased in size, from

40-foot wells to 45, 48, and now 53 feet (to match increased container lengths), in five- and three-car articulated versions as well as stand-alone cars.

Articulated spine cars are another popular intermodal car, as they are lighter than flatcars and can carry either containers or trailers.

Intermodal traffic was dominated by piggyback into the 1980s, but the advent of double-stacks led to containers overtaking piggybacks by 2000. Today, intermodal represents about a third of all rail traffic, with container traffic being about 85 percent of intermodal.

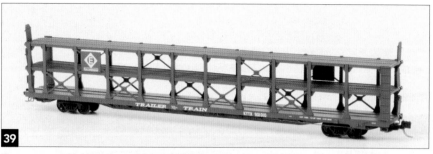

39

Open auto racks were used from 1960 through the mid-1970s. This is a Micro-Trains N scale 89-foot tri-level car with a 1960s TTX scheme and Erie Lackawanna rack.

40

Enclosed auto racks were developed to deter vandalism, and began appearing in the 1970s. This N scale 89-foot tri-level car wearing Southern colors is from Micro-Trains.

41

Center-beam cars carry bundled lumber. Some cars have a girder-style beam. This HO model is a 63-foot "opera-window" style Thrall-built car from ExactRail.

More information

25 Freight Car Projects (Kalmbach, 2016)

Detailing Projects for Freight Cars & Locomotives by Pelle K. Søeborg (Kalmbach, 2013)

Done in a Day by Pelle K. Søeborg (Kalmbach, 2009)

Freight Cars of the '40s and '50s by Jeff Wilson (Kalmbach, 2015)

Guide to North American Steam Locomotives, Revised Edition, compiled by George Drury (Kalmbach, 2015)

The Model Railroader's Guide to Diesel Locomotives by Jeff Wilson (Kalmbach, 2010)

The Model Railroader's Guide to Freight Cars by Jeff Wilson (Kalmbach, 2005)

Flatcars

Flatcars carry almost anything that won't fit into an enclosed car. Many are fitted with customized racks for carrying specific lading. Lumber, industrial machinery, vehicles, electrical transformers, pipes, boilers, and farm implements are just a few common loads.

By the early 1900s, a typical flatcar was 42 feet long, with a steel frame covered by a wood-plank deck. Size grew to 50 and 53 feet by the 1950s and 60 feet by the 1960s, along with the 85- and 89-foot piggyback flatcars discussed earlier. A common variation is the bulkhead flatcar, with end walls to keep loads from shifting.

The auto rack evolved in the 1960s, using the 89-foot flatcar designed for piggyback service. This car saved the automobile market for the railroads: loading was cumbersome with 50-foot boxcars, and trucks were taking away much of this traffic. Early auto racks had open construction, with two or three decks for vehicles, **39**. Due to damage from vandalism, enclosed cars began appearing in the 1970s, **40**.

A center-beam variation was developed for the lumber industry, **41**. These bulkhead flats have a center wall or beam framework that allows loads of packaged lumber to be secured to the center. They became popular in the 1970s and 1980s.

Another specialty flat is the coil-steel car, which first appeared in the late 1960s. These have cradles or saddles down the center of the car to carry thin sheet metal rolled into coils. Removable covers (two on early cars; one on most modern cars) protect the coils.

Today, flatcars of all types account for about 12 percent of the total freight car fleet (193,000 cars).

Stock cars

Stock cars are now extinct, but they were common from the steam era through the 1950s. They carried livestock (mainly steers, pigs, and sheep) to market, generally from ranches and farms in the West to large stockyards and packing plants in the Midwest. Stock cars look like boxcars but have open slatted sides for ventilation.

Railroads operated significant numbers of stock cars in the early 1930s (about 97,000 in 1932), but trucks began eating into the market (especially short- and medium-haul traffic) shortly thereafter, and packing companies began building plants closer to areas where stock was raised. The number of stock cars dropped to 54,000 by 1941 and to 31,000 by 1960. Other than a few dedicated service routes, rail transport of livestock was largely gone by the mid-1970s.

1

CHAPTER SEVEN

Benchwork

Beginning modelers sometimes overlook the importance of solid benchwork in the excitement of getting their trains running and models built, **1**. Good benchwork doesn't have to be complicated or time consuming, but rushing through construction or using inadequate or poor materials will lead to a wobbly structure, operating troubles, derailments, and frustration.

The benchwork on Bob Lawson's HO Southern Railway layout flows smoothly around his basement. Whether large or small, and regardless of scale, benchwork must be built solidly to support a layout. *Lou Sassi*

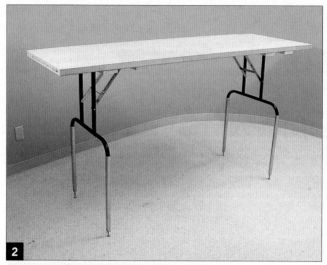

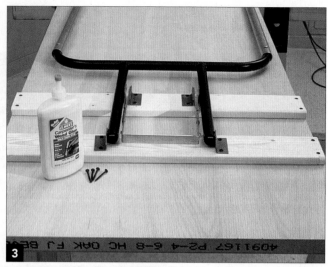

2 Among the simplest designs for table-style benchwork is a hollow-core interior door using either a frame with legs or folding legs. Folding legs can be extended with lengths of PVC pipe, metal pipe, or conduit. *Jim Forbes*

3 Glue and screw 1 x 4s across the door to provide a solid base for the folding legs. The screws must go into the door's outer frame. *Jim Forbes*

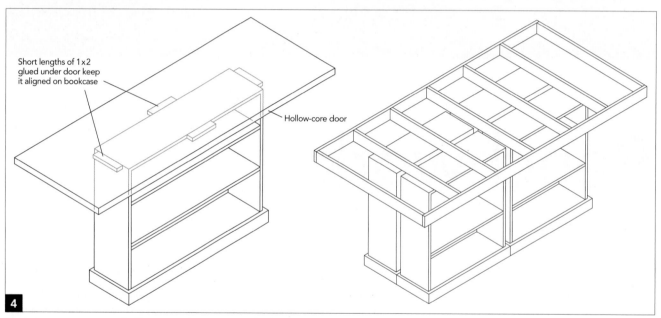

Short lengths of 1 x 2 glued under door keep it aligned on bookcase

Hollow-core door

4 Bookcases can support hollow-core doors or standard benchwork grids.

Benchwork is the full support structure for a model railroad. It includes the basic framework, legs, bracing, and table—everything below the scenery and track. As you'll see, benchwork can be very simple and utilitarian, or it can be quite fancy. The approach is up to you.

Benchwork can be freestanding, attached to walls, or a combination of the two. Construction style falls into two types: grid or L-girder, with the top surface either open or covered (tabletop). Most benchwork uses a combination of dimensional lumber

and plywood, but extruded foam insulation board is also popular.

The type of benchwork you choose depends on the size and style of your layout: Is it an around-the-walls design, with or without peninsulas? Is it a freestanding, island-style layout? Do you want to be able to move it at some point?

Let's look at the advantages and disadvantages of various types of benchwork, and examine a few examples. You can adapt these techniques and styles to your particular situation.

Tables and islands

As explained in chapter 2, many modelers start out with small table-style layouts (and many never go beyond that point). An advantage of a freestanding table is that you don't need to drill holes in walls or block anything along a wall.

Among the easiest types of tables to build uses a common hollow-core household door. These doors are lightweight compared to plywood, yet they're strong and relatively inexpensive. They're 80" long (6'-8") and available in 18", 24", 28", 30",

Layout height

Layout height is a much-debated topic. The overall trend is toward tall layouts, where viewers see scenes at or near eye level while standing for realistic views that replicate what we see in real life. Layouts that are too tall, however, make it difficult for working on scenery and track (especially far from the layout edge) and can make it a challenge for shorter people to reach in to uncouple cars or throw turnouts.

For shelf or around-the-walls layouts where operators walk or stand with their trains, consider a height around 46"–50". For a table, consider that same height or one a few inches lower if operators will sit on stools. You should, of course, adjust the height to suit your own preference.

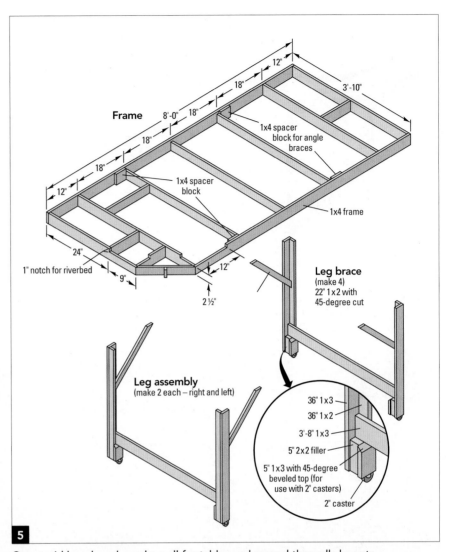

Open-grid benchwork works well for tables and around-the-walls layouts.

32", and 36" widths. They're typically 1¼" thick, made of two thin sheets of lauan plywood, with solid dimensional lumber around the outside of the door.

They are especially handy for N scale, where you can do a complete loop on a 28"- to 36"-wide table, or for HO or larger layouts where you don't need a turnback loop (such as an industrial switching layout). You can also put two loops end to end, in an L shape, or side by side to expand the space.

The basic idea is shown in photo **2**. You can build dimensional-wood framework with legs, or you can mount two pairs of folding table legs under the door, **3**. (You can buy them from home centers and websites, or scavenge a set from an old folding table.) Since these doors are hollow, the backing plate needs to be screwed to the outer edge where the solid wood is located.

Table layouts (hollow-core doors or grids) can also be placed atop bookcases, **4**. A single bookcase will support a door, and two bookcases back to back will support a 4-foot-wide layout. Multiple bookcases can be placed side by side for along-the-walls layouts. Bookcases look good, are solid, eliminate a lot of framework construction, and provide storage space.

Frame and grid

The traditional option for table and larger layouts is an open-grid design, with framework and legs for bracing. There are a number of ways to do this, but a good basic grid design is shown in figure **5**. The principle is simple: a grid of 1 x 3s or 1 x 4s supports the table, with legs made of an L (a 1 x 2 glued and screwed to a 1 x 3) and braced by 1 x 2s.

You can also use 2 x 2s for legs. An advantage of L-design legs is having increased stability in both directions, so they require less angle bracing. This design works for tables to 6 feet wide and 10 feet long; larger tables will need additional legs.

The benchwork built from the drawing shows why the various small cross members were added to the grid, **6**. You'll have to do this based on

where you need various components to match your track plan design.

An around-the-walls grid works in similar fashion, and peninsulas can easily be added at any point, **7**. Simply keep extending the grid and add pairs of legs every 6 to 8 feet.

These designs show legs with rolling casters, a good choice for a table design that makes it easily portable. Another option for table layouts is adding adjustable feet to the bottoms of the legs, **8**. The feet make it easy to adjust leg height to compensate for uneven floors. For permanent layouts, you can just cut and adjust each leg to the exact height needed.

A good rule-of-thumb with grids is to make sure the table or subroadbed is supported every 14"–16". Add additional cross members if needed (you

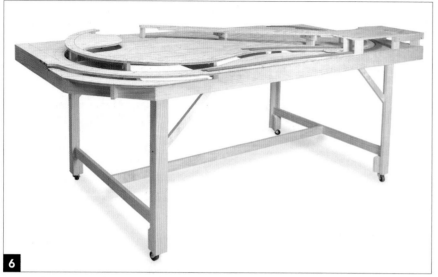

can do this later, when adding roadbed and other tabletop components).

L-girder

An alternative to open-grid designs is L-girder benchwork, so named because the main supports are two L-shaped girders, **9**. The girders are made by attaching a horizontal 1 x 2 atop a vertical 1 x 2, 1 x 3, or 1 x 4, **10**. Screws driven upward through the 1 x 2 flange hold cross members in place, **11**. The girders make the design extremely strong. This design works with widths up to 5 feet and lengths up to 20 feet possible with just four legs. The legs can be attached in the same way as with grid benchwork.

Horizontal joists (1 x 3s, or 1 x 4s for tables wider than 4 feet) are placed

6 Here's the open-grid benchwork as illustrated in figure 5, with a cookie-cutter plywood top and lengths of boards (risers) holding up parts of the top that are elevated from the grid. *Bill Zuback*

7 Hans Nicolaus used open-grid benchwork for his around-the-walls layout, which also includes a peninsula at one end. Hans added his backdrop to the wall; you can also add support posts to the benchwork to support the backdrop. *Horst Meier*

8 Adjustable feet make it easy to account for uneven floors when building table-style layouts.

9 L-girder benchwork features two lengthwise L-shaped runners, with cross members (joists) atop. The joists can be any length, making it a good option for layouts with curved edges. *Dick Christiansen*

Benchwork tools

Invest in a good drill-driver and a set of twist drills. A reversible drill/screwdriver bit speeds many jobs, and spade bits in ½" and ¾" sizes are also handy.

Power saws are very useful, including a handheld jigsaw (saber saw), circular saw, and—if you have the space—a power miter saw.

Depending upon where you live (apartment, condo, or house) and how much room you have, you may be limited in the type and number of tools you can have and use. If you own only one power tool, make it a good-quality cordless drill-driver. It's amazing how many holes need to be drilled (and screws driven) in even a small table, and a good drill-driver will make short work of it.

Choose one with a ⅜" chuck. You'll find 9-, 12-, 18-, and 24-volt versions. In general, the larger the battery pack and higher the voltage rating, the more torque it will have and the longer the battery will last.

Buy a basic set of twist drills, like the ones shown, that includes bits from ¹⁄₁₆"

through ⅜". You can buy larger bits as you need them, such as ½" and ¾" spade bits that are handy for drilling access holes for wiring.

Power saws are handy but not absolutely necessary. Most home centers and lumberyards will cut dimensional lumber and plywood for you (usually for a nominal fee). A power miter saw is useful if you have the space for it. It works quickly and provides square, clean cuts. A handheld circular saw is versatile, as it can make straight cuts in plywood and square or angled cuts in dimensional lumber. A saber saw (handheld jig saw) is perfect for cutting curves in plywood or hardboard. It can be used for cutting dimensional

lumber as well, but it takes longer and the cuts won't be as precise.

Handheld crosscut saws will do the same tasks as power saws, but using them takes more time and effort, and they're not as precise. A miter box and saw provide precise cuts with dimensional stock.

You'll find clamps essential for holding things together during assembly. Quick-release bar clamps (such as Quick-Grips) are my favorite—they adjust, clamp, and release quickly, and are available in several sizes. Common C-clamps are also handy.

Other tools I consider essential include a tape measure, hammer, screwdrivers (standard and Phillips), and a sanding block with various grits of sandpaper.

10 Make the girder by gluing and screwing a 1 x 2 flange atop the vertical girder.

11 Fasten each joist by driving a screw upward through the flange in the L girder.

Ryan Moats' layout provides a good illustration of cookie-cutter construction. The plywood table surface is cut with a saber saw, with portions raised and lowered on risers as needed. *Ryan Moats*

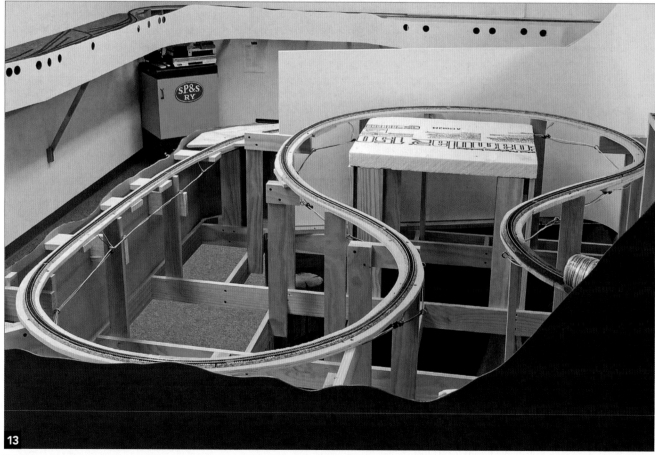

If hills or mountains will cover the benchwork, just cut the subroadbed and attach it to risers. Sheets of foam or plywood can be added to support buildings or towns.

Basics of wood

At the top are a Select-grade 1 x 4 and 1 x 2; at the bottom is a No. 2 and Better 1 x 4.

Plywood is made by combining three or more thin layers of wood, glued so the grain runs perpendicular between layers. At the bottom is ⅛" tempered hardboard, which is good for backdrops and fascia.

Most types of benchwork require some type of wood, including dimensional lumber, plywood, and composite materials such as hardboard. You can buy lumber at home building centers as well as traditional lumberyards and dealers (your best choice if there's one nearby).

For benchwork, choose kiln-dried, nontreated pine or fir dimensional lumber. Common sizes for benchwork include 1 x 2, 1 x 3, 1 x 4, 2 x 2, and 2 x 4. (Note the lack of inch marks, as the actual dimensions are smaller. For example, a 1 x 4 is not 1" x 4", but rather the planed/sanded dimensions (¾" x 3½") of a rough-cut board.)

Lumber is sold by quality in three main grades: Select (the best; boards are knot-free and straight), No. 2 and Better (some small knots; boards may have some bows in them), and No. 3 (larger knots; boards are often bowed or twisted). Select is the most expensive and No. 3 the cheapest, and as the saying goes, you usually get what you pay for.

Select boards are terrific to work with—use Select lumber (especially for smaller layouts) if you can possibly afford it. If not, go to No. 2 and Better, but only if you can hand-pick the boards (if you order wood for delivery, you're at the mercy of what the dealer picks for you). You can usually find boards in this grade that will work for benchwork.

Avoid No. 3 lumber. The knots often compromise strength, and warped and twisted boards make it very difficult to assemble benchwork that stays square, straight, and true.

Plywood is made of three or more thin layers of wood glued together, with the grain on each layer running at right angles to each other. Thin plywood (¼" and ⅜") works well for vertical faces and sheathing (backdrops, fascia, doors and covers), but it is too thin for tabletop (unless covered by foam) and track surfaces. For these, use ½" or ⅝" (some modelers opt for heavy ¾" material).

Common pine or fir plywood is fine for most benchwork uses. Check the grade: A is the best (smooth; with knots filled) and D the roughest (unsanded; knots not filled). Each side is rated, so you generally need only one good side (the top), making A-C grade a good choice. Plywood is also rated as interior or exterior—choose exterior if possible, so any exposure to water (scenery processes, etc.) won't cause the wood to weaken or delaminate.

Hardboard (Masonite is one brand) is a dense, pressed fiberboard that is tempered (hardened) on one or both sides. It works well for backdrops, control panels, fascia, and other vertcal sheathing but not as a table surface.

Another sheet material you'll often find referenced regarding benchwork is Homasote. This is a light-density fiberboard used in construction for sound insulation. Many modelers use it for roadbed, as it's light enough to push nails and track spikes in with pliers, but dense enough to hold them securely. It can be difficult to find in many areas—check homasote.com for information.

across the tops of the girders, spaced 14"–16" apart. They can be placed at angles to make way for below-track features such as rivers. Secure them with screws from under the L flange, **11**.

Remember the "⅕ rule" with L-girder benchwork: each pair of legs should be placed ⅕ of the distance in from each end, and the girders should be placed about ⅕ of the way in from the ends of the cross members.

For girders, 1 x 2 verticals are sturdy enough for lengths up to 8 feet, 1 x 3s up to 14 feet, and 1 x 4s up to 20 feet. For long girders, use splice plates of the same size boards as the girder. I recommend splice plates 12" to 14" long (four times the depth of the web is a good guideline), glued with wood glue and secured with at least five screws on each end.

14

Extruded foam boards can be used as table surfaces, either by themselves or atop a hollow-core door or sheet of thin plywood. *MR staff*

15

By using two or more layers of foam, it's easy to carve contours for details below track level. *MR staff*

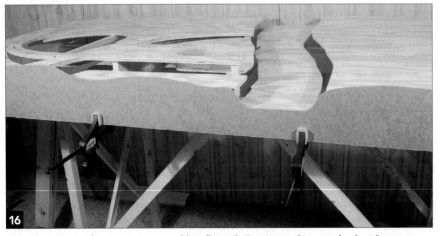

16

This fascia is cut from ⅛" tempered hardboard. Fascia can be attached with screws into the edge girder (open grid) or the joist ends (L-girder).

Make sure web and flange joints are staggered.

As with open-grid, the L-girder design can be adapted to around-the-walls designs (even wall-mounted), including peninsulas.

Layout tops and subroadbed

Whether you use grid or L-girder as a framework, how you proceed with the layout surface and track base (subroadbed) is a matter of personal preference and the type of scenery you're modeling. If you're modeling a large urban area with no grade changes, or relatively flat territory, you can simply use plywood or foam as a table across the entire benchwork surface.

Cookie-cutter tops are an excellent option, and very versatile, **12**. For this, cut sheets of material (plywood or foam) to allow for raising or lowering the track grade and to allow features placed below the surface, such as lakes and rivers. The elevated portions are supported by vertical wood risers (lengths of 1 x 2s, 1 x 3s, or 1 x 4s) screwed to the grid or cross members.

You can also leave the benchwork open and add just the subroadbed atop the grid, using ½" or ⅝" plywood cut slightly wider than the cork roadbed, **13**. This works well for mountainous areas or rural areas with lots of hills, as the scenery would cover up a tabletop anyway. You can merge this with a cookie-cutter style at town and city areas.

Foam and plywood

Foam and plywood each have their advantages and disadvantages as layout surfaces, and both have their dedicated fans and followers.

Sheets of extruded foam are sold as insulation in thicknesses from ¾" to 2". As a stand-alone table surface, use at least a 2" sheet, or layer two or more sheets atop a ¼" plywood table, **14**. By layering boards of various thicknesses, foam allows you to combine benchwork with scenic contours (see more in chapter 10), **15.**

Foam's big advantage is that it's easy to cut without power tools, using a serrated knife or hot-wire foam tool. Disadvantages are that it

A simple black curtain hung behind the fascia creates a very clean, neat look on Larry Nast's HO layout. *Dave Rickaby*

A simple bracket of 1 x 2s or furring strips supports a backdrop (hardboard in this case). The bracket can be wall-mounted or mounted to the layout itself.

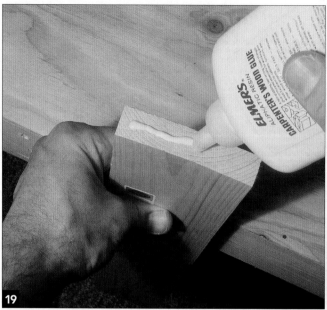

For grid joints, run a bead of wood glue on the end piece and then use two or three screws to secure it. Make sure the alignment is square.

can be challenging to mount under-table switch machines on foam, and track nails won't hold securely to the material.

Plywood is strong, versatile, easy to glue, and—with proper tools—easy to cut. It will hold track nails securely, and adding below-table switch machines and other devices is relatively simple. However, plywood sheets can be a challenge to handle, and apartment dwellers are limited in their use of power tools.

Avoid MDF (medium-density fiberboard), OSB (oriented-strand board), and particle board. Both MDF and particle board are susceptible to moisture and not as strong when cut into narrow strips, as for subroadbed. With all three of these materials, it can be difficult to drive in track nails and spikes.

Fascia and backdrops

As many photos throughout this book show, having a smooth front face on your layout is much more attractive than seeing the ends of boards. You can cut fascia from thin plywood or tempered hardboard such as Masonite. It can be glued, nailed, or screwed in place to the side girder or the ends of cross members, **16**. You should paint it either black or a dark green that matches your overall scenery color.

You can do more by covering the entire front of the benchwork. An inexpensive way to do this is taking black muslin, available at fabric stores, and mounting it with hooks or Velcro, which provides you with easy access behind it, **17**.

Any layout that's viewed from only one side will benefit from a backdrop. Even a simple flat board, painted sky blue, is much better to look at than a bare concrete or plasterboard wall, and you can later paint and detail it (see chapter 10).

As with fascia, any smooth, thin, sturdy material will work, such as hardboard or heavy sheet styrene plastic (at least .080" thick). Thin plywood can also be used, but the grain may show through the paint. Installing the backdrop early in the process—before adding the tabletop or subroadbed—is easiest, **18**.

Construction tips

As you assemble benchwork, use glue and screws for most wood joints, **19**. You can use either drywall screws or conventional flathead wood screws (I use no. 8 screws in lengths from 1¼" to 2"). Although drywall screws often don't require a pilot hole, they can sometimes split dimensional lumber on the end. When using them with plywood, you'll get a cleaner finish

with a pilot hole. A reversible bit/driver allows you to quickly drill a pilot hole, then flip the bit and drive a screw.

Make sure all cuts are square, and that joints are square and aligned before adding glue or screwing parts into place. For framing, use two screws for 1 x 2s and three for 1 x 3 and larger pieces.

Benchwork should be level. Leveling a freestanding layout or table can be a challenge—remember that floors, especially in basements, often tilt or slope.

Most importantly, work safely. Use care when using a power tool or cutting tool, and always wear safety glasses, even when using hand tools. A mishit nail or broken screw can easily go flying, and even a handsaw makes dust that can irritate eyes.

More information

Basic Model Railroad Benchwork, Second Edition, by Jeff WIlson (Kalmbach, 2012)

Building Frame Benchwork from Start to Finish (video), Model Railroader Video Plus (kalmbachhobbystore.com)

Building L Girder Benchwork (video), Model Railroader Video Plus (kalmbachhobbystore.com)

CHAPTER EIGHT

Track and roadbed

Good trackwork is the key to smooth operation regardless of the scale you're modeling or the size of your layout. Properly aligned track joints, smooth curves, and track that's in gauge (especially at turnouts) will ensure trouble-free operation. Modelers also want track that looks realistic, **1**.

The two main goals of model track are smooth operation and realistic appearance. Using realistic-size rail, painting the rails and ties, and adding ballast all help make it look like prototype track.

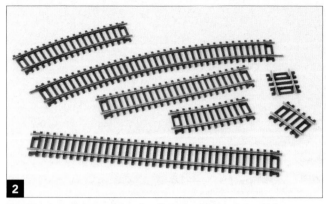

2

Sectional track is available in all scales (this is Atlas HO code 83). It is made in a wide variety of lengths and curve radii.

3

All-in-one track includes an elevated ballast profile. These HO sections include (from bottom) Atlas True-Track, Kato Unitrack, Bachmann E-Z Track, and Walthers/Life-Like Power-Loc.

4

Flextrack (bottom) has gaps in the tie strip, which allows the track to be curved.

5

HO flextrack includes, from bottom, Atlas code 83, Atlas code 100, Walthers code 83, and Atlas code 83 with concrete ties.

Track basics

Track includes the rails, ties, and other hardware such as spikes and tie plates. The sidebar on page 69 explains the various components and details of prototype track.

Most model track on the market today features nickel-silver rail on plastic tie strips, with wood grain, spike, and tie-plate detail molded in place (model track with concrete ties is also available). This combination of components works well, and the track is impervious to any moisture produced from adding scenery and ballast.

Brass rail (identifiable by its bronze color) was common in HO through the 1990s, but I suggest avoiding it, as the oxide that forms on it is nonconductive, requires frequent cleaning, and can cause electrical interruptions. Also avoid steel rail (used by some manufacturers for sectional or train-set track), which is difficult to cut.

Just as prototype rail varies in size, model track in N through O scales is available in multiple sizes. Regardless of scale, model rail is measured in code, which is simply the rail height in thousandths of an inch. For example, common sizes in HO include code 83 (.083" tall rail) and code 100 (.100" tall). The chart on page 68 shows how rail codes in N through O scales relate to prototype rail sizes.

Types of track

Model track is divided into three basic categories: sectional, sectional with built-in roadbed (all-in-one), and flextrack.

Sectional track is made in rigid pieces, or sections, of various lengths and curve radii, **2**. The most common radii for HO are 18" and 22" and for N, 9¾" and 11", although broader curves are also available. The tie strip is notched under each rail at each end, allowing stamped-metal rail joiners to

be slid in place to join sections. Typical lengths for straight sections include 6" for N, 9" for HO, and 10" or longer for O scale (with many smaller "filler" sizes). The number of curved sections it takes to form a complete loop varies by radius and scale—usually 12 or 16 pieces.

Sectional track's main advantage is its ease of use. Its main disadvantage is that curves are rigid—you're locked into only what manufacturers offer. You're also somewhat limited by the lengths of track offered, but as you'll see, track is easy to cut to custom sizes.

All-in-one track is offered by several manufacturers in each scale, **3**. This type of sectional track has a molded plastic base that simulates the ballast profile and texture of prototype roadbed. With some brands, the roadbed is molded with the ties; for others, the roadbed is separate and can be removed if needed. Roadbed color varies by manufacturer.

As with standard sectional track, all-in-one track is available in several curve radii and in many lengths, although some lines are limited in offerings. Be aware that each manufacturer uses its own type of connectors, so unlike standard sectional track, you can't easily combine multiple brands of all-in-one.

All-in-one's main advantage is that separate roadbed and ballast aren't needed, which offsets some of the additional cost of all-in-one track. Disadvantages are the same as sectional: no variation on curve radii and limited lengths (and it's more difficult to cut or modify, especially turnouts). You'll find some track arrangements like parallel sidings, yard ladders, and some junctions difficult or impossible to do with the turnout designs of some lines of all-in-one track.

Looks can also be an issue. The appearance of all-in-one track ranges from "not bad" to extremely toy-like—and you'll pay higher prices for the best-looking versions. However, there are things you can do to the roadbed to dress it up, including painting it and adding separate ballast.

Flextrack is also available in all scales, and it's the track of choice for most serious modelers. This track has gaps in the tie strips between some ties, which allows the track to be curved, **4**.

Its chief advantage is that it can be curved to almost any radius desired. Also, flextrack is made in long strips (usually 30" to 39"), which eliminates many intermediate rail joints—and

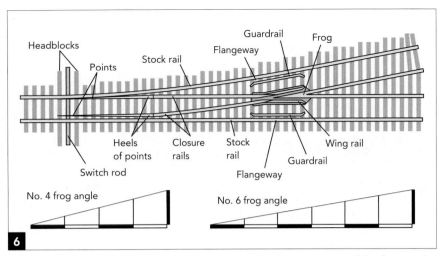

6 Turnouts are made of various parts. They are sized by the sharpness of the frog angle.

rail joints are track's main source of electrical and operational problems.

The disadvantage of flextrack occurs when bending curves: one rail will always be longer, so track must be cut. Making joints on curves can be tricky. Both of these become less of a problem with practice.

So which type of track should you use? If you're just starting out and building a small layout with a simple track plan, try standard sectional or all-in-one track. You'll have a chance to play with different track arrangements and get a feel for the tracklaying process.

If your track plan is a bit more complex (including a passing siding and a few spur tracks), go with standard sectional track, but get a couple of pieces of flextrack and experiment. You can use the flextrack for long, straight sections, and to get the feel for cutting

and fitting track, you could try laying a broad curve or two.

As you gain more experience, you'll likely find yourself gravitating to flextrack. Some modelers also opt to handlay track—building their own track in place using rail, ties, and other components. That's beyond the scope of this book, but something to consider for the future.

What track should you choose? Track lines differ in appearance and realism, **5**. I recommend sticking with the smallest commonly available size for your scale. Avoid code 80 track in N and code 100 in HO—both are grossly oversized, and the details themselves are heavy and unrealistic. Even if you don't notice this now, you probably will later. Smaller, finer track is durable, as long as you take care when laying it and aren't heavy-handed when cleaning it after installation.

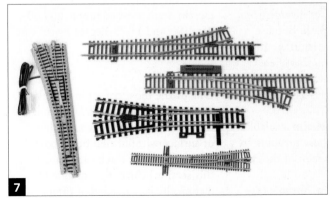

7 Turnouts include, clockwise from left, Kato N Unitrack remote-control left-hand no. 6, Atlas HO Snap-Switch code 83 in left and right (with manual controller), Atlas Code 100 wye, and Atlas code 55 N left no. 5.

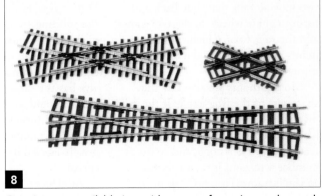

8 Crossings are available in a wide range of crossing angles, such as these HO pieces: a Walthers 30-degree crossing, an Atlas 45-degree crossing, and an Atlas 19.5-degree crossing.

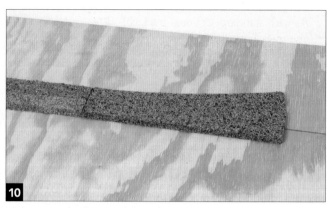

Run a bead of white glue along one side of the track centerline and then press the cork strip in place. Push pins will hold it in place until the glue dries.

Midwest and others make preformed pads for turnouts. You can also cut your own from larger sheets of cork.

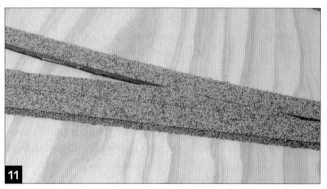

At turnouts, lay the two outside strips first. Follow by cutting and fitting the two inside pieces. Don't worry about small gaps—just make sure the surface is level.

Smooth any rough edges along the cork with sandpaper (a sanding block works well).

Turnouts

Turnouts (also called *track switches*) are track sections that allow one route to branch into two (or three). Standard turnouts have a main route (straight) and curved route (diverging).

You can see the various parts of a turnout in figure **6**. Key parts to know are the *frog*, which is where converging rails meet at an angle; the *points*, the two moving rails that slide back and forth to guide wheels to the two routes; and the *switch rod*, which connects the points and slides back and forth to throw the turnout.

Most turnouts are sized by the sharpness of the frog angle: if the rails diverge 1 scale foot in 4 feet of length, it's a number 4 turnout; 1 foot for 6 feet of length is a no. 6, and so on. A number 4 turnout is relatively sharp, so you'll want to use no. 5 or no. 6 turnouts if possible. (This applies to all scales.) Turnouts measured this way have rails that are straight at the frog, so be aware that they cannot simply

be dropped into a circle of track and fit properly.

Exceptions to the "number" measurement for turnouts are Atlas Snap-Switches and Peco's radius turnouts, which have curved diverging routes through the frog and are intended to replace curved track sections, **7**.

Another type of turnout is the *wye*. With a wye, both routes diverge from the entering straight path. Because of this, the numbering is different: the track angles of a no. 2 wye are equivalent to a no. 4 standard, a no. 3 wye has the same angles as a no. 6 standard, and so on.

Curved turnouts are also available. Instead of numbers, these turnouts are usually labeled by the radii of the two curves.

As chapter 9 explains, turnouts are available wired as all-live or in power-routing fashion. All-live turnouts require no special wiring, and I recommend them for most applications.

Crossings

Crossings allow two routes to cross each other at grade. No special wiring is involved—commercial crossings include hidden jumpers that route power around insulated frogs where rails of each route meet, **8**.

Crossings are measured by their angles. A wide variety is available in most scales: 90-, 45-, and 30-degree crossings are most common, and 60-, 25-, 19-, and 11.25-degree pieces can also be found.

Roadbed

One of the most common mistakes made by beginners is to lay standard track directly on the layout table or surface without roadbed (those using all-in-one track can ignore this section). Although roadbed technically isn't needed, it offers several advantages. It elevates the track above the surrounding landscape, just like the real thing, making track more realistic. It provides a good

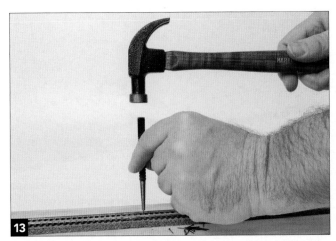

13 Use a nail set to finish driving the track nail into place. Keep the nail set vertical, and use small taps until the nail is in position.

14 Leave a paper-thin gap between the nail head and top of the tie. This is Atlas HO code 83 sectional track.

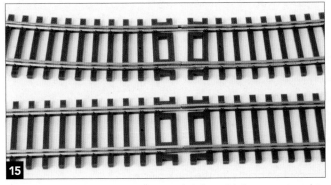

15 Make sure rail joints are square and tight, with just a paper-thin gap between rails (bottom). Misaligned joints, like the curves at top, will lead to derailments.

16 Use needlenose pliers to push a spike into place through the hole in the tie next to the rail.

contour for the application of ballast, which also improves realism. It makes operation quieter by getting trains off of the wood or foam surface (which can act as a sounding board). And it provides a smooth, solid, even platform for track that smooths out any imperfections in the foam or wood sub-base.

The most common roadbed material is cork, which is inexpensive, easy to use, and readily available in all scales. Made by Midwest Products and others, it comes in 3-foot-long strips and is perforated at an angle down the middle. Pulling the pieces apart, flipping one side over, and butting the pieces together provides roadbed with an angled shoulder on each side.

Before adding the roadbed, you should have already test-fit your track. If you're fitting complex combinations of sectional track, take photos of the final arrangement with a camera or cell phone so that you can refer to it later. Mark the track locations with a centerline as a guide for roadbed.

On a wood base, run a bead of white glue on one side of the centerline and press a cork strip in place, **9**. On a foam base, use Woodland Scenics Foam Tack Glue. Push pins (or map pins) will hold the cork in place until the glue dries.

Repeat the process with strips on each side of the centerline. Stagger the joints so they aren't parallel. Make sure the strips are pressed firmly to the surface and tightly against each other. A utility knife works best for cutting cork. (You could use a hobby knife, but the cork will dull the blades rather quickly.)

For turnouts, premade turnout pads (from Midwest and others) are easy to use, **10**. You can also cut your own turnout pads from large sheets of cork (the large sheets are also handy for yards and large areas of complex trackwork). You can also cut and piece strips together, **11**. Start with the two outside

pieces and then cut the inside strips to fit. Don't worry about small gaps or imperfections—ballast will hide these. Just make sure that the surface is level.

When the glue dries, remove the pins. One edge of the cork will have a rough burr along the top edge—remove it using a sanding block with 120-grit paper, **12**. Feel along the roadbed for any bumps or undulations, and sand these down as well. Then you're ready to lay the track.

Laying track

The three main ways to secure track to roadbed are using small nails (brads), small spikes, or glue. Most lines of sectional track (including all-in-one) and some brands of flextrack have two or three holes in the middle of their ties (at each end and in the middle) for placing track nails. Using nails works well for sectional track in all scales and for all track in N scale, where driving individual spikes is difficult.

17 Push the spike against the tie/rail base by closing the jaws of the pliers and pushing downward. The spikes along the rail provide a better appearance than nail heads in the middle of ties.

18 Use a putty knife to spread adhesive in an even, thin coat along the top of the roadbed.

19 Press the track firmly in place in the glue. Make sure joints are snug and properly aligned.

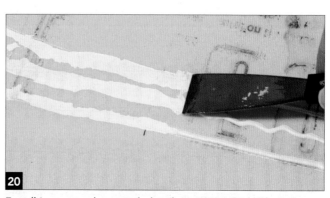

20 For all-in-one track, spread glue (here, Foam Tack Glue) along the contact points for the track pieces.

Walthers (Shinohara) HO flextrack and turnouts (and some other brands) have small holes in the ties next to the rails that are designed to hold small spikes.

Gluing works well for sectional or all-in-one track, but you'll want to be certain of your track arrangement because later adjustments are difficult to impossible to make. Glue is good for foam surfaces, where spikes and nails won't provide a strong hold.

Let's start with track nails. Don't use common wire nails. Atlas and others make small, black round-head brads,

and the black color helps hide them from view when installed. Start at a piece of track in a central location and work outward. A turnout is a good starting spot.

Hold the track section in place and insert a nail into a hole, pressing it down through the roadbed. Use a small hammer to tap it until the head is just above railhead level. Then, use a nail set to finish driving the nail until the head is just above the top of the tie, **13**.

Keep the nail and nail set as straight and vertical as possible. Use gentle taps—don't try to drive the nail all at

once. Also, stop driving the nail just before it contacts the tie, **14**. Driving it farther can buckle or kink the tie and distort the track. If you accidentally bend a nail, pull it out with a wire cutter and swap in a new nail.

Once the first piece is in place, just add the next. Slip two rail joiners on the rail ends and carefully slide the two pieces together, making sure a rail didn't slide over the joiner. As chapter 9 explains, it helps to know where to install insulated rail joiners or joiners with feeder wires attached—this will save you trouble later.

Push the new section tightly in place, then pull it back just slightly (no more than ⅓₂") to allow a bit of room for expansion and contraction of the roadbed and subroadbed. Nail this section as you did with the first one and then continue the process. Make sure all joints are square and tight, **15**. Kinks (especially on curves) will lead to derailments.

When you get to the last three or four sections that finish an oval or loop, put all the sections in place, making

Rail sizes

| | Prototype rail in pounds | | | | | | |
	70	90	100	110	132	155	*180
N scale code				40		55	*80
HO scale code	55		70		83	100	
S scale code	70	83		100		125	
O scale code	100		125		148		

*Oversize—rail this heavy was never used by prototype railroads

Prototype track

Prototype track has a tall profile atop ballast roadbed.

Most track consists of steel rail spiked to tie plates and wood ties.

Concrete ties, with rails secured by clips, are now common on main lines.

Prototype track consists of lengths of steel rail laid on crossties made of wood or concrete. Everything is secured by spikes and tie plates, and ties rest on a bed of crushed rock called *ballast*.

Let's start with rail. The wide part at the top that supports the wheels is the *head*, the vertical portion is the *web*, and the wide, flat part at the bottom is the *base*. Rail is unpainted, so it quickly weathers to a rust color of light to dark brown, with a shiny steel railhead where wheels polish the surface.

Rail varies in size (measured by its weight in pounds per yard) depending upon usage. Modern mainline track is typically 132-pound rail (standing almost 7" tall); mainline track in the early 1900s used 80- or 90-pound rail (5½" tall). Sidings are often 100- to 120-pound rail (6" to 6½" tall).

Wood ties are the most common. Modern ties are 8½ to 9 feet long, 7" tall, and 9" wide. They are pressure-treated with creosote or other preservatives, giving new ties a dark brown to black color which tends to fade to medium and light gray after

years in the elements. Steel tie plates rest between the rails and ties, with spikes holding the rails and plates in place.

Concrete ties began appearing in significant numbers in the 1980s, and can now be found on many heavy-duty main lines. These are 9 feet long, 9" tall (with a depressed area in the middle), and 11" wide. The rail rests on a tie pad, with clips or fasteners that clamp the rail base in place.

Ties rest on a bed of crushed-rock ballast, which provides drainage and spreads the weight of the track structure. Ballast profile is tallest on main lines and shallower on sidings, branch lines, industrial tracks, and seldom-used lines. Some spur tracks and older branch lines have little or no ballast.

Ballast, in turn, sits atop a graded subroadbed. The subroadbed has a well-defined profile on heavy main lines, but may not be as prominent on secondary lines and branches. The key is that the roadbed is above the surrounding landscape, which provides adequate drainage and support for the track structure.

sure joints fit properly, and then nail them in place.

Using track spikes is a bit trickier, but the appearance is more realistic. Lay sections in the same fashion but use needlenose pliers to push a spike in place, **16**. Finish driving the spike by closing the jaws of the pliers and pushing the spike until it rests against the rail base, **17**.

When using either spikes or nails, wear safety glasses. These tiny, sharp parts can easily go flying out of pliers or a mis-struck hammer.

Gluing track

Glue holds track firmly in place, and it has the advantage of not having any visible spikes or nails. Be certain of your track arrangement before gluing your track because, once the glue dries, it will be almost impossible to salvage the track if you need to change anything.

I've had good luck with Liquid Nails for Projects, a water-based construction adhesive. It's fairly thick, spreads well, and allows a bit of working time before setting. Work one or two track sections at a time, running a thin bead of the adhesive down the center of the roadbed.

Use a putty knife to spread the adhesive in a thin layer—no more than 1/32", **18**. It doesn't take much to firmly secure the track, and a thick coat will ooze up through the ties when the track is laid in place.

Attach rail joiners, insert a new section into the joiners, lower it to the roadbed, and press it down firmly, **19**. Make sure it's aligned properly. If the track starts to buckle up, or doesn't set firmly in the adhesive, press a map pin between ties in the middle to hold it.

For turnouts, keep glue away from the points and throw bar. I usually only glue a few ties at each end, just in case

I need to make any adjustments later. Use a track nail or spikes if the turnout needs to be held down in the center.

If something goes amiss and you need to remove glued-on track, work a putty knife under the ties and try to work the track up slowly.

All-in-one track can be glued in place in a similar manner. Spread a thin layer of adhesive on the subroadbed or table and then add each piece of track, making sure it is pressed firmly in place, **20** and **21**. Weights atop the track will ensure that it lays flat.

Fitting track

You'll eventually find that you need a piece of track in a length that isn't offered commercially (or that you just don't have on hand), or you'll need to cut flextrack to fit. It's an easy task to cut track with rail cutters, **22**. These look like common wire cutters, but the blades actually pass by each other,

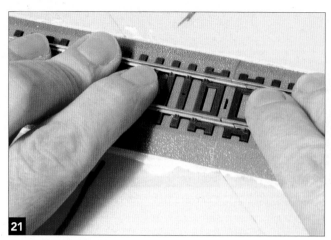

Press the track in place on the glue. You may have to add weights atop the track to hold it firmly until the glue sets.

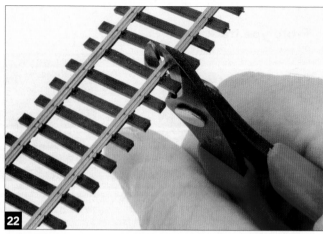

Xuron rail cutters make quick work of cutting rail. The rail to the left of the cutter will have a square end.

A couple of passes with a flat file ensures that the rail end is square.

Lay the first piece of flextrack on the curve, leaving the last couple of inches straight. Cut the rail ends so they are square.

cutting in a shearing motion. This leaves one end of the rail square.

Mark the top of each rail with a fine-point marker and then use rail cutters to trim each rail. Give the rail end a few passes with a flat mill file to make sure there are no burrs or rough edges, **23**.

You'll also have to cut one or two ties from the cut end of the track to allow room for a rail joiner. Save the ties—you can add them back under the track joint after the track is in place (trim the spike and tie plate detail away with a hobby knife to clear the rail joiners).

Flextrack

You can lay flextrack with any of the above tracklaying methods (although glue can be tricky with long sections). Trim rails as needed, making sure that joints are square and tight. The only

real trick is joining flex track on curves. The process is the same regardless of scale.

Bend the track to shape around the desired curve. Some track, like Atlas Super Flex, flexes very easily; other brands have to be worked slowly. Trying to bend it too quickly can damage track by breaking off spike heads and pulling out the rail. Make sure that the curve is smooth and not a series of jogs and sharper angles.

When the first curved piece is ready, spike it in place, but don't secure the last 3" or so—leave it straight. Trim the long rail so the rail ends are even, **24**. Add the next section of track, making sure the joint is square with no kinks.

Solder the joint to secure it, **25**. (See chapter 9 for details on soldering.) Hold the iron where the rail ends and joiner meet, and touch the solder to

the outside of the rail at the rail/joiner joint until the solder begins to flow. Then remove the iron and let the joint cool.

You can now continue flexing the next piece of track to fit, **26**. Use a small flat file on the top of the rail to make sure that the joint is smooth, **27**. Add a couple of scrap ties under the rails at the joint and glue them in place before ballasting the track. Leave a small rail gap at the first joint in a straight portion following the curve (no more than 1/16").

As you install track—especially turnouts and crossings—test-run equipment frequently to make sure everything works properly. This means more than rolling a boxcar along the track. Clip a few temporary wires to the track and run several locomotives back and forth, especially through each route of every turnout. Also run

25

Solder the joint. Hold the iron to the rails and joiner, and touch the solder to the joint away from the iron until the solder flows.

26

Continue laying the track with the following section, flexing it to a smooth curve.

27

File the top of the rail at the joint to ensure that it is smooth.

28

Caboose ground throws are easy to install at the end of a turnout throw bar. This is an HO version.

a six-axle diesel or your biggest steam locomotive. Now is the time to find any problems, so they can be fixed before you paint and ballast the track.

Controlling turnouts

Most brands of turnouts are available in either manual or remote-control versions, with higher-quality turnouts available only in manual versions (many experienced modelers choose to add their preferred brand of controller).

Turnouts need some type of mechanism to hold the points securely in position. Most all-in-one turnouts have a slide switch on the side that slides the points back and forth (as do many remote-control turnouts with side-mounted switch machines). Micro Engineering turnouts have an internal spring that holds points in position.

For other turnouts, if you don't use a manual or powered mechanism, passing train wheels will eventually bump them out of position, and lead to a derailment.

A *switch machine* is an electrically powered device used to throw a turnout. Turnouts sold as remote control have built-in (usually side-mounted) twin-coil switch machines controlled by push button (or combination slide switch/push button) switches. Pushing the button for each route powers a magnetic coil, which snaps the points into position for that route. The control switch can be placed on a control panel or on the layout's fascia at the track location. Follow the manufacturer's instructions for wiring.

Advanced modelers often choose under-table switch machines for a clean appearance. These switch machines can be controlled by switches on a control panel, on the layout front or fascia, or remotely with a Digital Command Control stationary decoder.

For now, stick with manual controls. You can always add under-table remote-control machines later, but if you think you might want to do this, do a bit of prep work. When laying track, prior to spiking each turnout in place, drill a hole through the roadbed and subroadbed directly between the rails under the center of the turnout throw bar. Use a 3/16" hole for N scale and 3/8" in HO and larger scales. This will provide access later for a control rod passing through the roadbed from an under-table switch machine.

Caboose Industries makes an extensive line of ground throws that are rugged, dependable, and easy to install and use, **28**. Some even include a rotating indicator target. They're slightly oversize compared to a prototype switch stand, but their other qualities make up for that.

Gaps and feeders

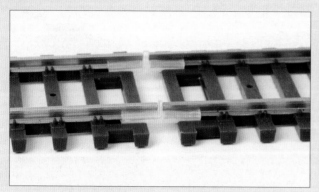

Insulated rail joiners should be used at all locations that require a rail gap for wiring.

Rail joiners with feeders are easy to install. Drill a hole under the rail at the feeder location.

Chapter 9 will explain about where you need to gap rails and add feeder wires for controlling trains, but knowing where gaps and feeders are needed **before** laying track makes the job much easier.

Insulated rail joiners are made of plastic (left photo). They keep rails aligned like metal joiners do, but they include a vertical plastic piece to keep rails from bumping into each other.

Atlas and other companies make metal rail joiners with feeder wires attached (right photo). The feeders can then be soldered to the track power bus (main supply wires).

Ground throws vary by the length of travel required for the turnout throw bar. Use the smallest ground throw that works for your turnout. To determine this, simply measure how far the throw bar travels from side to side on your turnout.

Follow the Caboose instructions for mounting the ground throw. The company offers a variety of connectors, or you can attach them by simply

drilling a matching hole on the end of the throw bar. I recommend choosing the sprung version of the appropriate ground throw.

You can also make a simple, inexpensive manual turnout control with a piece of piano wire (steel wire) or a simple metal paper clip, **29**. Bend it to shape as shown in the photo. Then insert the long end into a matching hole drilled two ties away

from the throw bar, and the short end into a hole in the center of the throw bar, **30**.

You'll have to adjust the exact dimensions to suit each turnout installation, which can simply be done by bending the clip angle. As you slide the points back and forth, the spring will at first resist, but then it will snap the points into the opposite position.

NMRA gauges

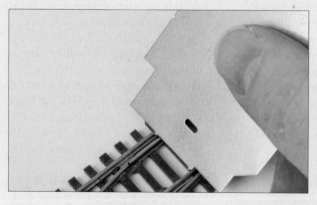

The National Model Railroad Association makes standards gauges for most scales and gauges, including N, HO, HOn3, S, Sn3, O, and On3. The instructions list all the functions; most valuable are the tabs

that show if track is in proper gauge (left photo) and the notches that indicate if wheels are in proper gauge (right photo).

If you're having problems with derailments, examine the track at that spot. If

multiple cars or locomotives have issues at the same spot, it's probably the track; if the same car or locomotive derails in multiple locations, check that car's wheels.

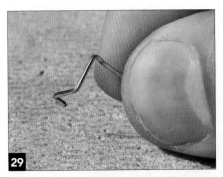

29 For a simple manual turnout mechanism, bend a piece of steel wire or a paper clip into a spring in the shape shown.

30 Insert the long end of the spring into a hole drilled into a tie. The other end goes into a hole centered in the throw rod.

31 Testor's paint markers work well for painting rail and ties. Use various rust colors, applied in layers.

32 You can also paint ties and rail with a brush. Place several drops of different colors in a small lid and then vary the colors as you apply them.

33 Railheads should be clean and shiny. Clean paint and grime with an abrasive track-cleaning block such as a Walthers Bright Boy.

Painting track

A simple way to greatly improve your layout's realism is to paint the track and ties. Model rail is bright, shiny nickel silver; look at prototype rail and you'll see many shades of rust, brown, and black. Model tie strips are molded in either black or brown plastic, which tends to have an unrealistic plastic sheen compared to the real thing.

A great way to paint the track and ties is with Testor's CreateFX enamel paint markers, **31**. Testor's set no. 73801 includes all the colors you'll need: rail brown, rail tie brown, and rust. Start with the ties. Give each tie a quick swipe with either of the brown markers. Give some ties a second coat, and vary the colors to create a more realistic look.

For the rails, pick a color and give each side of each rail a coat. Work slowly, so the paint works around the spike and tie plate detail at each tie. The color won't cover completely,

which is good: You can now take another color and go over the first coat, creating a varied effect. I like starting with rust, a bright color, and finishing with the darker brown colors, letting some rust highlights show through.

The spikes can chew up the felt tips on these markers. Testor Corp. sells replacement tips for the markers, and it's smart to have a few spares on hand.

You can also use standard hobby paints to paint track. Use a brush and various rust, roof brown, and rail brown colors, **32**. Make sure you use flat, not gloss, colors for the most realistic effects.

Cleaning and ballasting

As you paint track, some paint will inevitably get on the tops of the rails. Remove this as soon as the paint dries using a Bright Boy or other track-cleaning block, **33**.

Maintaining clean track is vital to good operation. The best way to

keep track clean is by running a lot of trains. You'll find that if you don't operate trains for awhile, dust, grime, and oxidation will begin to affect locomotives. If you notice locomotives stalling or stuttering, give the rails a quick pass with a track cleaner.

You can ballast track at this point, but many modelers will wait until the scenery is done (or in progress) before ballasting to avoid having stray plaster, Sculptamold, or grass fibers make a mess of it. We'll look at ballasting track in chapter 10.

More information

Basic Trackwork for Model Railroaders, Second Edition, by Jeff Wilson (Kalmbach, 2014)

Building a Model Railroad Step by Step, Second Edition, by David Popp (Kalmbach, 2012)

CHAPTER NINE

Control and wiring

Cody Grivno runs a train with a wireless Digital Command Control (DCC) throttle on David Popp's N scale layout, as Mike Polsgrove tracks cars in the yard. DCC has made it easier than ever to have two or more operators simultaneously running trains on a layout. *David Popp*

Being able to run model trains—and doing so in a realistic fashion—is what sets model railroading apart from other static-model hobbies, **1**. Being able to run two or more trains at once has never been easier with the growth of Digital Command Control (DCC). Some basic electrical and control knowledge will get your trains running in short order.

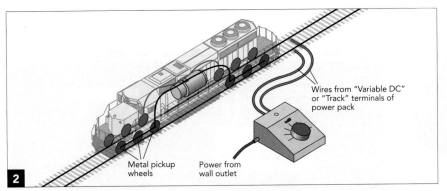

2

A power pack supplies DC to the rails—positive to one rail and negative to the other. Reversing direction is a matter of changing polarity via the direction switch on the pack.

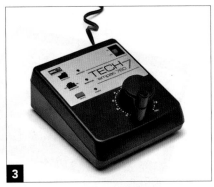

3

This MRC Tech 7 is a modern power pack that includes momentum and brake controls and a voltage-regulation feature. *MRC*

4

Power packs include output terminals for track power (variable DC) and one or two sets of accessory outputs (both AC and DC on this pack). This pack is rated at 16 volt-amps.

Electrical controls and connections for operating trains and accessories is known as wiring. Wiring can be quite simple for a small layout, such as a single controller and two wires to the track. It can become more complex for larger layouts, or for small layouts on which you want to operate two or more trains independently of each other. We'll look at several ways of doing that, but first, let's cover some basics of electricity and see how model locomotives and other accessories are powered.

Electrical basics

Electricity is measured in volts (V) and amperes, or amps (A). The lines that deliver power to houses and businesses are rated in thousands of volts; a typical neighborhood power line carries 2.2 kilovolts (2,200 volts). A transformer mounted on a pole outside your house steps the electricity down, with the electrical outlets in your house providing 120V.

5

The Prodigy Advance2 is an entry-level DCC system from MRC. From left are the command station/booster, tethered cab (throttle), and power supply. *MRC*

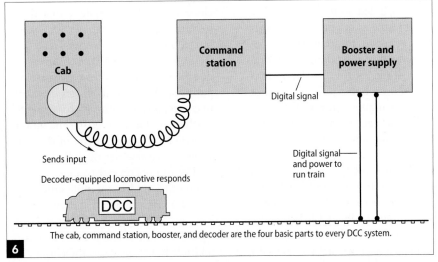

6

The cab, command station, booster, and decoder are the four basic parts to every DCC system.

In a DCC system, one or more cabs send signals to the command station. The command station groups the signals and sends them to the booster. The booster sends the power and digital signals to the tracks, where decoders respond only to signals intended for them.

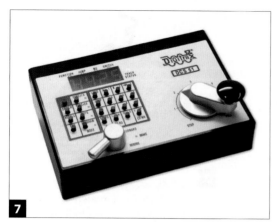

7

The Digitrax Zephyr (DCS 51) is an all-in-one entry system with a built-in controller. Additional tethered cabs can be plugged into the system. *Digitrax*

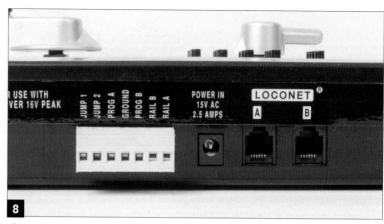

8

The rear of the Zephyr is simple—phone-style jacks for connecting throttles (or additional jacks), as well as connections to the layout track and a separate programming track.

9

Manufacturers offer a variety of handheld throttles, from simple to complex. These include the Lenz LH200, MRC Prodigy Advance, NCE PowerCab, Digitrax DT400, and NCE Power Pro. *Larry Puckett*

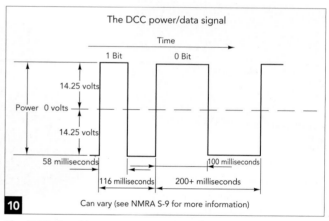

10

The DCC signal is square-wave AC, with messages communicated by the width of the pulses, which are variable.

Electrical devices draw varying amounts of electrical current, measured in amps, based on the amount of energy it takes to operate a device. A large motor, for example, one on a basement sump pump, might draw 8.0A, while a 40-watt incandescent bulb draws about 0.3A, although both are receiving the same 120V.

Because our trains (and their related motors and bulbs and accessories) are small, they are designed to run on much lower voltage and current than household devices. Model railroad control devices step the household 120V down to about 12–16V.

Current draw for most model devices is under 1A, so we often specify current in thousandths of an amp, known as *milliamps* (mA). Thus a motor drawing 0.3A draws 300mA, and a microbulb drawing .01A draws 10mA.

Household electricity is alternating current (AC), meaning that the electrons rapidly alternate in direction (60 times a second in the U.S.). Scale model trains run on direct current (DC), where electrons flow in one direction (technically from negative to positive polarity). This makes it easier to control a locomotive motor or switch machine motor, as reversing the motor direction is a simple matter of throwing a switch that reverses the polarity.

The motors on most modern locomotive models are quite efficient. A typical HO engine will draw 0.5A or less, and an N scale model draws 0.3A or less. Adding a sound decoder and multiple lights increases the current draw, but still usually under 1A for HO and smaller scales.

With either AC or DC circuits, a key is to keep each polarity leg separate, or a short circuit will occur. Shorts will shut down systems, and they can damage power packs, decoders, and other electrical components. A short circuit can occur in obvious fashion, such as dropping a screwdriver across the rails or running a locomotive over rail gaps between two blocks of opposite polarity.

They can also be less obvious, such as two uncovered solder joints under the layout accidentally touching each other or a metal uncoupling pin falling off a freight car and lying across the rails at a turnout. Be sure to keep all wiring neat and keep metal tools away from the track to minimize the chances of short circuits.

How do you use this knowledge to get a train rolling down the track? There are two systems for controlling scale model trains: conventional DC control with a power pack and Digital Command Control. Let's start with a look at conventional control.

Power packs

Into the 1990s, almost all scale trains were designed to run with low-voltage DC supplied by a power pack, and this is still a viable control system today, **2**. A power pack is a self-contained unit that plugs into a wall outlet, **3**. Inside, a transformer converts the 120V house current to low voltage (12 to 18V), and a rectifier converts the AC to DC. Two wires go from the power pack to the track to supply electricity for locomotives.

A dial (knob) controller simulates the throttle by adjusting the output voltage; the changing voltage regulates a model locomotive's motion from stopped to full speed. A direction switch reverses the polarity of the DC output, controlling forward and reverse direction. Some power packs have additional controls, such as an on/off switch and a power indicator light.

Advanced packs include momentum and brake controls. When momentum is switched on, it simulates the advanced time it takes to start and stop a prototype train—turning the pack to half power will result in slowly building up speed to that point. Pressing the brake switch will gradually reduce power, simulating a brake application, until the switch is released. The speed will then gradually increase back up to the throttle setting.

Modern power packs have microprocessor control, with potentiometers for speed control and integrated circuits and other devices for regulating output voltage. You don't need to know the technicalities of this, but what it means in practical terms is to avoid buying older or used power packs. Many power packs (especially small ones supplied in train sets) through the 1980s used rheostats instead of potentiometers for speed control, and they won't work well with today's low-current-draw motors.

Power packs vary in the amount of current they provide to run trains. Small train-set packs typically have enough power for a single engine. Larger power

Decoders must be programmed with a unique address. Do this on a separate programming track—specifics vary by manufacturer. *Jim Forbes*

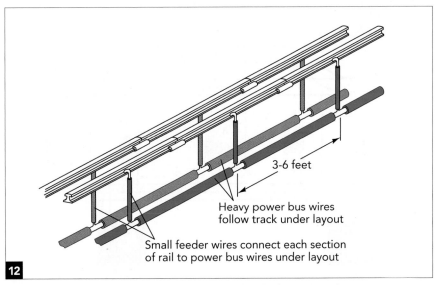

12

3-6 feet

Heavy power bus wires follow track under layout

Small feeder wires connect each section of rail to power bus wires under layout

For reliable DCC operation, run a track bus under the layout (two heavy power-supply wires) following the track, with feeders to rails every 3 to 6 feet.

packs can provide enough to power a train with two or three locomotives. Manufacturers include MRC, Dallee, MTH, and Atlas.

To check the current, see the pack's maximum output, listed in the instructions or printed near the output terminals. This is usually listed in volt-amps (VA). Divide the volt-amps by the top output voltage to get the current rating. For example, if a power pack is listed at 20VA, dividing this by a top output voltage of 12V gives a 1.7A rating—enough to power three locomotives drawing 0.5A.

Power packs have two or more sets of output terminals, **4**. The pair labeled *Variable DC* or *Track* are the throttle-controlled lines to the track for the trains. The pair labeled *Accessory AC* is a set-voltage AC output, usually around 16 to 18V (the exact voltage is labeled on the pack), designed for switch machines and other accessories. Some packs include an additional set of terminals labeled *Accessory DC* as well.

Although you can indeed use these outputs for accessories, it's a good idea to power these with a separate electrical supply. Especially with

13 Socket panels are placed around the layout, enabling throttles to be plugged in at multiple locations. These are connected to the command station with phone-type cables.

14 Here's a rear view of a socket panel. Most use phone-type connectors that allow them to be daisy-chained together.

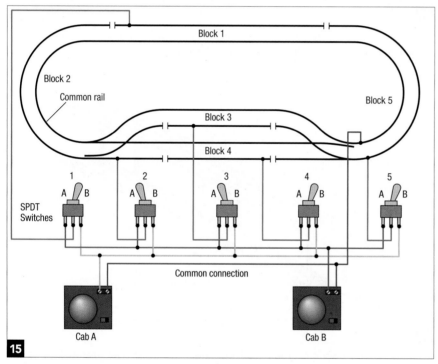

15 With cab control, the layout is divided into electrical blocks. A toggle switch for each block selects which power pack is in control of that block.

Conventional DC control

The advantage of using a power pack to control trains is that it's simple and inexpensive: hook up two wires to the track (one wire is positive and the other is negative), and you're ready to go. For larger layouts, you might need to run another set or two of wires to get power to distant areas of the layout. On a small layout, or any layout where smaller power packs, you'll find that accessories may use enough power to cause your trains to slow down.

you only intend to run one train at a time, this is all you really need.

The disadvantage comes as soon as you want to run two trains at once; say, having a friend run a freight train on the main line while you switch cars in a yard. The power going to the tracks from the power packs is indiscriminate: any train on the tracks will respond to the controls and start moving, so you can't simply add a second power pack.

To run two or more trains, you must begin dividing the track electrically into sections (called

blocks), with insulating gaps in the rails between blocks, and use toggle or rotary switches to regulate which blocks receive power from which power pack.

We'll look at that idea, called *cab control*, in a bit. But if you're just getting started in the hobby, Digital Command Control is a much better, more efficient, and easier way to run several trains at once.

Digital Command Control

Digital Command Control is arguably the biggest revolution ever in model railroading. With DCC, you can control two or more trains independently on the same section of track without having to divide the track into separate electrical blocks.

The basic idea is that, along with power, a series of signals from multiple throttles or controllers are sent through the rails. These signals are picked up by an electronic decoder in each locomotive. Each decoder picks up only the signals intended for it, which allows independent control.

A development of early proprietary systems, DCC was adopted as a standard by the National Model Railroad Association in the early 1990s. Major manufacturers include CVP Products, Digitrax, Lenz, Loksound (ESU), Model Rectifier Corp. (MRC), NCE Corp., and SoundTraxx (decoders only).

When you buy a system for your layout, you're buying that

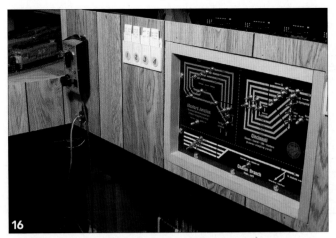

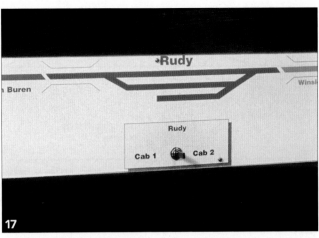

16 Control panels usually show a track diagram, with toggles located on the diagram to match the blocks they control. *Jim Hediger*

17 Panels can be localized, with switches located on the layout fascia near the blocks they control. *Mark Watson*

manufacturer's specific application of the DCC standard, so system components (throttle, command stations, boosters) must be from that manufacturer. However, any DCC decoder, from any manufacturer, can be used on layouts controlled by any other manufacturer's system.

Beginning modelers sometimes balk at the initial cost of a DCC system. However, the starter systems offered by most manufacturers have become reasonably priced, **5**. If you think that a basic DCC system is too expensive, start adding up the cost of the toggle switches, wire, control panels, a second power pack, and other components required for a cab control (not to mention the time that you'll spend doing the wiring)—and then remember that you can still only control two trains—and you'll find that the cost of a DCC system isn't as steep as you initially thought.

DCC components

A DCC system consists of one or more throttles (controllers), a command station, a power booster, a power supply, and decoders, **6**. Most manufacturers offer starter systems that look like a fancy power pack, with the command station, booster, and possibly a controller, all in one unit, **7** and **8**. This is a great way to get started in DCC, and for small- to medium-sized layouts, a starter system is all you'll ever need.

Each manufacturer offers multiple styles of handheld controllers,

from basic (speed and direction controls) to complex (full keypads for programming and controlling multiple decoder functions), **9**. Simple controllers provide an affordable alternative, with advanced controllers giving more features. You can add additional throttles as you need them (the maximum number allowed varies by the specific system). Throttles are either plugged into a jack or operate by wireless signal (radio or infrared).

The command station is the heart of a DCC system. The command station takes the instructions coming in from the throttles, converts the instructions to a digital signal, and sends it to the booster. The booster adds the power to the signal and forwards it to the track, where a decoder in each locomotive deciphers the digital signal, responding only to those signals intended for it.

You don't need to know this to run a DCC system, but the power sent to the rails is actually square-wave AC. Communications are indicated by the width of the wave pulses—a 1 is a short pulse and a 0 is a long pulse—Command strings are a series of 1s and 0s, making it a digital signal, **10**. Locomotive decoders rectify the AC into DC to power the motor.

Boosters are rated in power by amps. Basic systems usually have a 2A or 3A booster; larger systems range to 5A. You probably don't have to worry about anything larger right away, but most systems allow adding additional

boosters as needed (you always have a single command station). Add up the power being consumed by models at one time on your layout (including locomotives and lighted cars). If that approaches the current rating of your booster, you'll need to add another booster and divide your layout into two or more power districts. (*Wiring Your Model Railroad* by Larry Puckett, Kalmbach, 2015, contains more details.)

Most new locomotive models can be purchased with a decoder already installed (the easiest option); separate decoders can also be purchased and installed (see sidebar on page 82).

Decoders need to be programmed so that each has a unique address to receive commands. Decoders come from the factory preprogrammed to address 3—this needs to be changed to a two- or four-digit address. (Some systems only support a two-digit address; use a four-digit address if possible.) Simply using the locomotive number is the best method, as it's easy to remember. For example, locomotive no. 8084 gets address 8084 in a four-digit system or 84 in a two-digit system, and engine no. 923 would get address 0923 or 23.

Follow your system's instruction manual for programming decoders—it's a simple process, but the exact mechanics of doing so vary by manufacturer, **11**. Many other decoder functions can also be programmed and adjusted. Do this on a separate piece

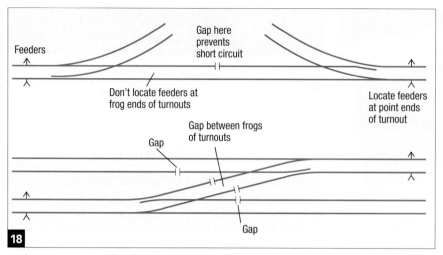

18

With power-routing (live-frog) turnouts, you'll need to add gaps between all frogs of opposing turnouts as shown. Also, always add track feeders on the point ends of turnouts, not off the frog ends.

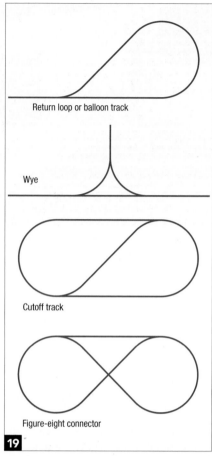

19

A reverse loop is any track combination that allows a train to turn back on itself.

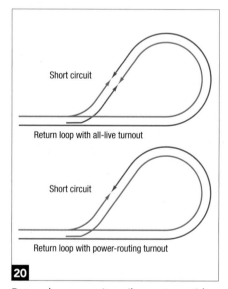

20

Return loops require rail gaps to avoid short circuits.

of track connected to the *Programming track* output on your command station.

Once a system is wired and in place, running trains is easy. Operators enter the addresses of the locomotive (or locomotives) to be controlled on their throttles. Advance the throttle, and your locomotives will start to move. Use the function keys to turn headlights on and off if needed, to blow the whistle or horn, or activate other effects on sound-equipped models.

You need to be conscious of turnouts: if you accidentally run into a turnout that's set for the other route, you'll create a short circuit. Systems are set to shut down automatically in case of a short. If you encounter one, clear the train (or other cause) and the system will reset itself.

Wiring a DCC layout

To install a basic DCC system, you'll need to connect the wires from the command station/booster to the track. To keep the signals to the track strong, it's a good idea to use feeders every 3 to 6 feet along the track, **12**. This is because nickel-silver rail is not a great conductor, and rail joiners are not always reliable.

Run two heavy wires (14AWG, or 16AWG for N or small layouts) from your system under the layout under the track. This is the *track bus*, the power supply for the track. Add feeders to the track from the bus, making sure you always feed the same rail from the

same bus wire. Color-coding helps keep this straight. For example, for a basic oval layout, make the inside rail red and the outside rail black.

(The following sections on turnouts and reverse loops will explain if you need to add any gaps in rails, and they include wiring tips for details on feeder installation.)

If you use plug-in throttles, you'll need to provide sockets along the edge of the layout for them (each manufacturer offers its own, and small panels with two sockets are common), **13** and **14**. These are typically connected by phone-style connectors and cables (but with six connectors instead of four) that are daisy-chained (one to another) with cable starting at the command station/booster. These cables make up the *cab bus*.

Wireless throttles require a receiver for your particular system. This is usually connected in line with the cab bus (see manufacturer's instructions for details).

This is obviously a very basic overview of DCC. For more detailed information, check out *Wiring Your Model Railroad* and *The DCC Guide*, both published by Kalmbach. Both books provide information on installing and operating a DCC system as well as programming and installing decoders.

Cab control

The alternate method of running multiple trains with standard DC

power packs is called *cab control*. Variations on this have been around since the early days of the hobby, and the basic concept is shown in figure **15**.

The idea is to divide the layout electrically into blocks. A toggle switch

Sound

Sound decoders have been available for a long time, but they have greatly improved in features, sound quality, and prototype fidelity in recent years. Gone are generic engine sounds, which have been replaced by sounds matched to specific prototypes (for example, an EMD 567 as in a GP7, or an Alco 251 as in a Century diesel). Sounds for specific horns are also available.

As with standard decoders, many locomotives are available factory-equipped with sound decoders, and manufacturers (in particular Loksound and Soundtraxx) offer a variety of sound decoders that can be added. Some

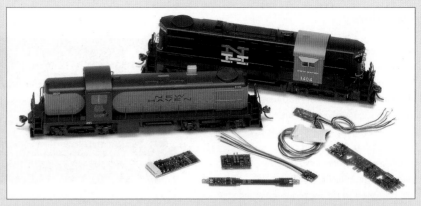

Locomotive decoders come in many styles, including circuit boards (drop-in replacements for models' original boards), plug-equipped, and wired. *Jim Forbes*

sound decoders include speakers; for others, you can choose and add speakers based on the size of the model you're

working on. Sound installations can be complex—letting the factory do it is the best solution for most beginners.

---

for each block allows you to select the power pack that will control any train in that block. As you run a train, flip the toggle switch for the next approaching block toward your power pack; when your train clears a block, flip it back to the center off position.

Blocks should be longer than your typical train length. Passing sidings should be their own block, as should mainline sections between the turnouts of passing sidings. Yard tracks should each be a separate block, and areas (perhaps an industrial track with several spurs) can be a single block. Any reversing loops or tracks must be a separate block.

The drawing shows common-rail wiring, where both power packs share one common return rail—one output wire from each pack goes to the common rail. This means only one rail requires gaps or insulated rail joiners between blocks.

Connect the other output from each pack to the terminal on the opposite side of each single-pole, double-throw, center-off toggle switch. The wire from the middle terminal of each toggle switch goes to its respective block. Color-coding wires helps tremendously in doing this.

Most modelers using cab control mount toggle switches on a control panel at a central location, **16**. Thin hardboard (such as Masonite) works

well for control panels, as it's easy to drill mounting holes for control switches. A great way to do this is to use a track diagram for the panel, and mount the toggles on the diagram to match the block they control, **17**. Power packs can be mounted on shelves on either side of the panel.

You can make a track diagram for the panel by drawing it with a graphics program on a computer and then printing it out. You can also use the traditional method of painting the panel white and applying thin masking tape to represent the track diagram. Paint the panel with a contrasting color (spray cans work well for this), remove the tape, and you'll have your track diagram.

Cab control is viable if you have a small layout and only plan to operate one or two trains at a time. Disadvantages include cumbersome operation—worrying about blocks and toggle switches instead of running trains—and lack of flexibility: you can only run two trains at once without expensive rotary switches or sub-blocks (which go beyond the scope of this book). Walkaround control is also difficult without additional wiring (having separate control buses for each throttle).

With the wide availability and ease of wiring and using DCC, I highly recommend that option to those just entering the hobby.

Turnouts

There are two types of turnouts: *all-live* and *power-routing*. As mentioned in chapter 8, all-live turnouts (often labeled as *DCC friendly*) have both routes coming out of the turnout live at all times. This is done by internal jumpers that connect rails on either side of the frog, so that the frog itself is not powered. This isn't usually a concern, as today's all-wheel-pickup locomotives can easily make it through the relatively short dead area of the frog.

Power-routing (also called *live-frog*) turnouts were quite common until about 10 years ago. With this type of turnout, the frog is always powered, and only the route selected is live. These turnouts require special wiring considerations.

Track lines with all-live turnouts include Atlas, Bachmann, Kato, Peco Insulfrog, and PowerLoc. The current Walthers line (made by Shinohara) has all-live turnouts (labeled DCC friendly), but until the early 2000s, Walthers turnouts were power-routing. Power-routing turnouts include Peco Electrofrog, Micro Engineering, and the older Walthers/Shinohara line.

For beginners, I suggest using all-live turnouts, as no special wiring is required for either conventional DC or DCC wiring.

Decoders

Most locomotive models are now available with factory-installed decoders, but there's a wide variety of aftermarket decoders available that modelers can install in locomotives that aren't already equipped. There are three basic styles: *drop-in*, *plug*, and *wired*.

Drop-in decoders (also called *plug-and-play*) are made to fit specific models, and are designed to be swap-out replacements for a model's original circuit board. These are usually quite easy to add.

Plug-equipped decoders are similar, but either fit into a socket on the circuit board or replace part of the circuit board. Installation is generally simple, but more work is sometimes required to fit the decoder in some locomotive shells.

Wired decoders are for locomotives without circuit boards or sockets. The motor must be isolated, and the decoder wired between the incoming track power

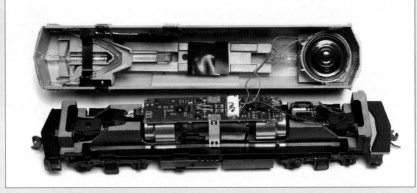

This is an HO Kato F40PH diesel fitted with a Digitrax sound decoder. The decoder is a swap for the model's original circuit board. The speaker fits in the rear of the shell.

and motor. Installation can be complex.

Decoders are rated by their rating in amps and by their number of function outputs. You'll need a minimum of two function outputs (one for front and rear headlights), with additional functions if you want to add a beacon or ditch lights. A 1A decoder is sufficient for N and Z,

with 1.25A-1.5A for HO and S, and 2A for O scale. Most decoder manufacturers have scale recommendations (and a list of models that decoders were designed for) listed on their websites.

(For details and instructions on installing decoders, see *DCC Projects and Applications, Volumes 2 and 3*.)

Wire

Insulated wire can be stranded or solid. In general, use solid wire wherever possible, but use stranded in locations where wire may have to move or flex repeatedly. Wire is commonly available as a single connector, with insulation in a variety of colors (handy for color-coding circuits), and in paired form (such as speaker wire).

Wire size is indicated by its gauge—in North America, it's American Wire Gauge, or AWG. The smaller the number, the heavier the wire. In model railroad terms, heavy wire is 12AWG and 14AWG— used for main power supply (bus) wires,

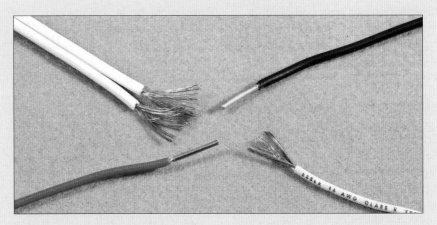

especially on larger layouts. Light wire is 24AWG to 20AWG, used for track feeder wires from main bus wires or wiring light-

duty circuits. Medium wire is 16AWG or 18AWG, good for power supplies on small or standard DC layouts.

If you use power-routing turnouts, you'll need to add gaps in some rails to avoid short circuits, **18**. The two basic rules when using power-routing turnouts are 1) Always add track feeders on the point side (not the frog side) of the turnout, and 2) Always include a rail gap where turnouts meet frog to frog.

Or better yet, just use all-live turnouts.

Reverse loops

To avoid short circuits, you need to be aware of reverse loops and reversing sections when designing a track plan and building a layout. A reverse loop is any track where trains can turn back on themselves, **19**. This means any trackwork that allows a locomotive to start on a section of track and wind up heading the opposite direction on the same track section.

Most reversing tracks are easy to spot; others can be disguised and harder to identify. The three most common types are a reverse loop, a wye, or a track that cuts back diagonally across an oval. All reverse loops require special wiring.

Every time a track turns back on itself, it creates a potential short circuit, as rails of opposite polarity meet each other, **20**. The solution is to use gaps in both rails to isolate the track within the loop or reversing section as a separate block and then use toggle switches or, for DCC, an auto-reverser to reverse the polarity in the block.

You can see two ways of doing this in diagram **21**: one uses a single double-pole, double-throw (DPDT) switch, and the other uses two switches. The single-switch method is best for DCC, while the two-switch method is best for standard DC.

Here's how it works: For DCC, make sure the toggle switch is thrown so that the reverse loop's polarity matches the route from the main line from which the train will enter the loop. Then, while the train is in the loop, throw the loop toggle switch. Since DCC isn't bound by plus/minus polarity for direction control, the train will continue running in the same direction.

For a standard DC layout, the two-switch method is best. Again, make sure the loop direction switch matches the main line. When the train is in the loop, throw the mainline direction switch. The train will continue running uninterrupted.

An option for DCC is to use an auto-reversing module, which can be wired between the track bus and the feeders for the loop section (in place of the toggle switch in the one-switch design). These sense the short circuit as a train enters and automatically change the polarity.

Wiring tips

Determine your wiring needs **before** you start laying track. This lets you know where you will need gaps in your rails early in the process. The easiest way is to add insulated rail joiners when laying track (see sidebar on page 72). To add a gap after track has been laid, use a cutoff disk in a motor tool, a razor saw, or a small hacksaw. Glue a small piece of styrene in the gap to make sure the rails don't touch if materials later expand or contract.

You'll need track feeders in many locations. Again, determining where these should be before laying track gives you more options. Atlas and many other companies offer rail joiners

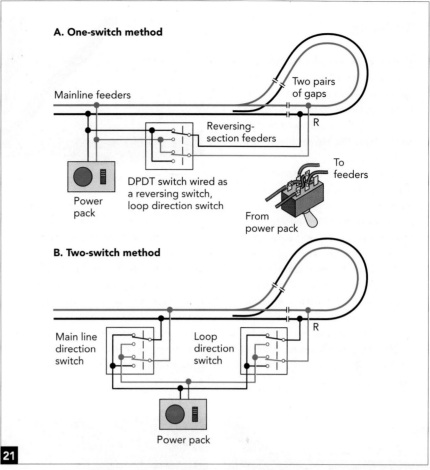

The one-switch method is best for DCC (or an auto-reverse module can take the place of the DPDT switch), and the two-switch method is best for standard DC control.

with track feeders attached to the bottom. Apply them like any other rail joiner and run the wire through a hole drilled through the roadbed and layout surface.

To add a feeder later, strip the insulation from the end of a length of appropriate wire (see the sidebar on the opposite page). Drill a hole through the roadbed next to the rail. It's safest to do this on the outside of the rail where it won't interfere with wheel flanges.

Bend the wire to an L shape so it will fit against the web and foot of the rail. Tin the wire by heating it with a soldering iron, and then touch the solder to the wire until the solder flows smoothly along it (see the sidebar on soldering on page 84).

Make sure the rail is clean. Scrape away any paint from the area, and buff away any oxidation with an abrasive track cleaner or wire brush. Tin this

area in the same manner as with the wire.

Run the wire through the hole and position it in place against the rail. Use a stainless steel tool (tweezers or a hemostat works well) to keep it from moving if necessary. Place a hot soldering iron over the joint until the solder on both surfaces melts and fuses together, adding a bit more solder if needed, **22**.

By doing this quickly, you can usually avoid melting adjoining ties. You can also add a heatsink on either side of the feeder by clamping a hemostat or placing a small wad of wet paper towel in place. Either will absorb excess heat before it gets to a tie.

Wires often need to be joined under the layout or behind control panels, and soldering will provide solid joints. Cover all joints with electrical tape or heat-shrink tubing to avoid short circuits.

Soldering

Soldering is a basic skill that you'll need to learn for installing many types of wiring, and you'll also need it for some trackwork. Get a good pencil-type soldering iron with a 30-watt or higher rating. Avoid the heavier trigger-style soldering guns.

Use stranded rosin-core solder. A 60-40 tin/lead content works well. The rosin in the core is a flux, which helps clean the joint to make the solder adhere firmly. You can also use lead-free solder. (Do not use acid-core solder, as the acid will cause joints to corrode with electrical contact.)

To solder a connection, you first need a solid wire joint. Strip the wire from the mating pieces of wire with a wire stripper. You can also use a knife, but be careful not to nick the wire, as this can weaken the wire, especially with small wire sizes.

Make sure that the wire is twisted securely; with stranded wire, make sure no stray strands are poking out. Hold the hot soldering iron so that it firmly contacts both wires. Apply the solder to the wires—not to the iron. When the wires become hot enough, they will melt the solder and it will flow into the joint. Remove the iron and then let the joint cool.

Cover the joints with electrical tape or heat-shrink tubing to protect the joints and eliminate the risk of short circuits from bare wires contacting each other. If using heat-shrink tubing, make sure you add the tubing before soldering the joint. After soldering, slide the tubing in place and hold the edge of the iron (not the tip) against it. It will shrink and secure itself firmly to the wire.

22 Hold the tinned wire against the rail with the soldering iron, adding more solder away from the iron.

23 With an insulation displacement connector, slip the connector over the main wire and the feeder wire in the slot. Use pliers to clamp the metal conductor in place.

24 Flip the cover in place and you're done. IDCs work best for track feeders branching off the power bus.

Mechanical connectors are also popular for many types of wire joints. Insulation displacement connectors (IDCs), also known as *suitcase connectors*, are handy for joints where a smaller wire branches from a main wire. They are quick to install, as no stripping of wire is needed. Their main use on layouts is for track feeders from the main power bus.

These are available from several manufacturers and in a variety of sizes (the wire sizes are listed on packaging and often the connector itself). I prefer 3M brand because the metal internal connector is U-shaped, which provides two connection points instead of one as with many other brands, **23**.

To use one, slip an IDC over the main (bus) wire and put the end of the stub (feeder) wire in the appropriate slot. Use square-jaw pliers to press the metal connector in place (the metal tab cuts through the insulation of the wire and just into the wire itself). The plastic hinge is then folded over the top of this tab and snaps in place, **24**.

Keep it simple

Wiring can be intimidating, but for small layouts, it's generally not a complex process. I recommend getting a copy of *Wiring Your Model Railroad*—it's a great reference book for both DC and DCC layouts, and it will help you troubleshoot any problems you might encounter.

More information

The DCC Guide, Second Edition, by Don Fiehmann (Kalmbach, 2014)

DCC Projects and Applications, Vol. 3, by Mike Polsgrove with Cody Grivno (Kalmbach, 2015)

Wiring Your Model Railroad by Larry Puckett (Kalmbach, 2015)

1

CHAPTER TEN

Basic scenery

Scenery is the most notable component of your model railroad, **1**. Even getting a basic coat of green turf atop a plywood or foam layout surface greatly enhances your layout's realism, **2**. But don't let adding scenery intimidate you—the basic techniques are simple, and scenery is easy to change and modify if you don't like the initial results.

Scenery turns a collection of models into a model railroad. Having features both above and below track level creates a dramatic effect, as Don Sauret accomplished with this scene on his HO Maine Central layout. *Don Sauret*

2

Even a basic layer of green ground cover and texture (at left) makes a dramatic difference in appearance, compared to bare wood and Sculptamold (at right), on Dave Fodness' HO Penn Central layout. *Dave Fodness*

3

Larry Over built an extensive cardboard web form to support the trackside foothills on his N scale Southern Pacific layout. *Tim Miller*

4

Andy Sperandeo covered his cardboard web with pieces of kraft paper to create a stronger shell. This also makes it easier to create precise landforms. *Andy Sperandeo*

5

You can give flatlands some relief or create rolling hills with crumpled newspaper and strips of masking tape.

Scenery consists of three basic steps. First comes the basic scenic shell or scenic contour. This initial step covers the benchwork and creates the overall shape of the landscape, such as hills, mountains, and riverbeds and lakebeds. It also provides bases for roads, streets, and structures. The second step is ground cover: simulated grass, weeds, dirt, and other colors and textures. The third stage is scenic details, such as trees, rocks, roads, streets, and water.

Have a solid plan in mind before starting the scenery process. Your track should already be in place. Outline other details on the layout, including streets, highways, structure locations, and rivers. The more levels of details you have above and below the level of your track, the more you eliminate the tabletop appearance—and the more realistic your

layout will be. As chapter 7 explained, this is why you need to consider scenery as you build your benchwork, especially for rivers, lakes, and cities.

Scenery offers more methods and materials for doing each step of the modeling process than any other area of the hobby. There are numerous ways of approaching scenic contours, many materials you can use for ground cover, dozens of ways of making trees, and several materials for making water. None is the "best" way—all are valid and have their own advantages and disadvantages. What works best for you will depend on the availability of materials, the type of scenery you're trying to create, and your personal modeling preferences.

Let's start with building scenic contours.

Web and shell

The most popular method—and an easy one—is the cardboard web, **3**. To do this, cut strips of heavy cardboard to 1" to 2" widths. Use hot glue to secure one end of several strips to the base of a hill. Add additional cardboard strips in a crosswise pattern, building up the web to the desired height and shape. Either hot glue or staples work well for securing the web.

These webs can be extensive or simple. For taller hills and landforms, use scrap pieces of wood or foam under the web to support it. Continue building the web until the shape is what you're looking for. You can cover this web with pieces of brown (kraft) paper, stapling or hot-gluing it in place, **4**.

A variation of this method, especially for low-lying or softly

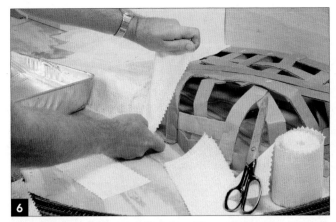

6 Cut plaster gauze into small pieces. Dip each piece in water and then apply it over the scenic form. *Jim Kelly*

7 Place one or two cups of Sculptamold in a plastic bowl. Slowly add water while stirring until the material reaches the consistency of paste.

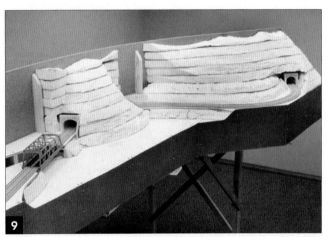

8 Spread a thin coat of Sculptamold over exposed plaster cloth and bare plywood to avoid dead-flat areas. *Jim Kelly*

9 Dick Christiansen layered foam board to create the scenery profile on his N scale Salt Lake Route layout. *Dick Christiansen*

rolling hills built atop a solid table, is to use wadded-up newspapers and masking tape. Simply crumple the paper and spread it to the basic form and then secure them with strips of tape, **5**.

With either of these methods, you then need to create a hardshell surface for subsequent ground cover. Before proceeding, consider covering your trackwork with masking tape to protect it from stray plaster and paint.

The classic method of making a shell is to mix plaster, dip strips of paper towels in the plaster, and then place them on the contour. However, this is a messy, time-consuming process.

An easier, faster, and less messy technique is to use plaster-impregnated gauze, which is available from Activa, Woodland Scenics, and others. It

comes in rolls, typically 6" wide. You can apply it in two ways. The most common is to cut it into manageable pieces (9" to 12" long), dip them in a shallow pan of water, and then place the pieces over the form, overlapping them slightly, until the contour is covered, **6**. The plaster cloth is thin, but it provides a remarkably solid base once it dries. One layer is usually enough, but two will produce an even stronger shell.

An alternate method is to first set the plaster-cloth pieces in place and then wet them using a spray bottle. The advantages to this are that you can use larger pieces and you don't have to worry about plaster dripping onto other surfaces as you apply the strips.

You then need to coat the plaster to provide a base for texturing. The traditional method again is plaster,

but a less messy alternative is using Sculptamold, a plaster product containing paper fibers. Made by Amaco, it's available online or in most hobby and craft shops. The fibers keep it together, making it less messy than plaster, and it provides a strong scenic shell.

In general, I use Sculptamold for most scenery, but I use plaster if I need an extremely smooth surface, such as a riverbed. Each can be applied over any common scenery surface, including bare wood, foam, cardboard strips, screen wire, or any other contour material.

To mix Sculptamold, place a cup or two of the material in a plastic bowl. Add water slowly and mix with a spoon until the mixture reaches the consistency of paste, **7**. The mix shouldn't be runny—it should hold

10

Foam can be cut and shaped with many hand tools, including a serrated knife, file, or rasp. *Bill Zuback*

11

Hot-wire tools provide clean cuts in foam. This hand tool with shapable wire is from Hot Wire Foam Factory.

12

Scenery materials and tools include matte medium, white glue, earth-tone paint, Flex Paste, alcohol, spray bottles, brushes, pipettes, and eye droppers.

13

Ground foam in various textures and colors, along with static grass, is the basis for most basic ground cover.

together firmly when scooped up with a spoon. Mix only what you can use in about 10 to 15 minutes of application time.

Spread the material with a spoon or spatula, working it into a thin layer, about ⅛" or so, **8**. You can smooth it with the back of a spoon, a flexible spatula, or your fingers. Wetting your utensils with water gives you a smoother surface.

Sculptamold is quite strong even in thin layers, so thicker applications waste material and increase the drying time. Continue applying Sculptamold until the area is covered. The material will set firmly in 30 to 45 minutes. Let it dry completely (when there are no cold, damp areas) before proceeding to scenic texturing.

You can color Sculptamold while mixing it, but it's not necessary, since you'll paint it later. The advantage to coloring it first is that if you drill holes in it for trees, any dust or exposed material won't be stark white. To color it, mix some of the flat latex paint you're using for scenery (more on that in a bit) with water (3 parts water, 1 part paint), then use the mix to make the Sculptamold.

Foam contours

Foam boards came into wide use as a scenic base starting in the 1970s, and some modelers use foam as a benchwork material as well.

Extruded foam insulation boards are commonly available in 1", 1.5", and 2" thicknesses from lumber and home

centers in sizes to 4 x 8 feet. Sheets are blue, pink, yellow, or gray, depending upon the manufacturer. Woodland Scenics also sells white foam sheets in a variety of thicknesses and sizes.

Foam's chief advantages are that it's light, it can be cut and shaped with a variety of hand tools, it won't warp, expand, or contract because of water or humidity, and sheets can cover a wide area.

Its main disadvantage is that it can be very messy to cut and shape, as bits of foam get everywhere (and static electricity makes them stick). It can also take considerable time to carve some types of contours.

Photo **9** shows the basic idea of building up layers and contours with foam. Start with the lowest level, such

14 Paint the surface (here, foam and Sculptamold) with flat earth-color paint. Foam brushes work well for this.

15 Sprinkle the first layer of fine ground foam in place. The cork area at left is a base for a structure.

16 Blend various colors of ground foam for a varied, unkempt effect, adding medium and coarse ground foam over the fine base.

as a riverbed or lakebed, and stack additional layers on top as needed.

You can cut and shape foam with a variety of tools. Avoid power tools: they will make a huge mess, and you risk melting the foam. A utility knife works well for thin sheets. A serrated kitchen knife works best for cutting sheets thicker than 1". You can take care of the resulting mess of foam bits with a shop vacuum or hand vacuum.

To shape hills, riverbanks, and other contours, use a long serrated knife, **10**. You can also use coarse files or rasps, such as a Stanley Surform tool. The

Surform tool works well for rounding hills and other areas.

Another good way to cut and shape foam is with hot wire tools, available from Woodland Scenics, Hot Wire Foam Factory, and others, **11**. These use a thin wire in a U-shaped handle. An electrical supply heats the wire, so it cuts through foam. Basic and advanced models are available. Advanced tools allow you to bend the wire to custom shapes when cutting ditches or other contours.

When using a hot-wire cutter, don't force the tool through the material.

Pull the tool through gradually, slowing down if you feel resistance. You'll need to go slower for thick and wide cuts, but you can go fairly quickly through thin sheets. Follow the manufacturer's instructions and recommendations regarding heat and settings. Also provide adequate ventilation and avoid breathing the resulting smoke from the process.

Be sure to use foam-compatible glues when securing foam sheets to a wood base or to other foam. I prefer Woodland Scenics Foam Tack Glue, and Liquid Nails for Projects is also a

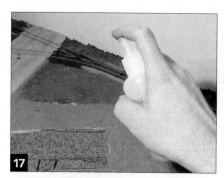

Soak the ground foam with alcohol or wet water, applied with a misting spray bottle or pipette.

Drip diluted white glue over the texture materials. The wetting agent will help it soak thoroughly into the materials.

Many static grass applicators use a battery, which requires a connection clipped to the wet-with-glue surface. Here, Tony Koester is applying long field grass to his HO layout. *Tony Koester*

Hold the Noch static bottle over the still-wet glue and repeatedly squeeze it while moving it horizontally around the surface. The fibers will stick to the glue and be pulled up toward the bottle cap.

Spread ballast along the sides of the roadbed and track and then down the middle of the track between the rails.

Use a soft brush to contour the ballast on the shoulders and spread it evenly between ties. Make sure all of the roadbed is covered.

good choice. Run a bead of adhesive on one mating surface and use a putty knife to spread it into a thin layer. Then position the piece and add weight on top until the glue sets, which can be a day or more, especially for large or wide pieces.

Another good option is latex contact cement such as DAP Weldwood Nonflammable Contact Cement. With contact cement, brush a thin coat on each surface. Let the cement dry several minutes (until it is dry to the touch), carefully place the top piece in position, and press it down firmly. The bond will be instantaneous, so make sure the pieces are aligned.

At this point, most modelers apply a thin coat of plaster or Sculptamold over the foam. It's not truly necessary if the contour is smooth enough, but it will even any rough areas or separations between foam sheets. You can also use Woodland Scenics Flex Paste or ready-mix spackle for filling small cracks and imperfections.

Ground cover preparation

The goal with ground cover is to provide texture and color that looks like real grass, weeds, soil, and brush. There are dozens of options for this. Ground foam has become the standard in recent years, and you'll find a variety of textures and colors from Scenic Express, Woodland Scenics, and others. Static grass has increased in popularity, and it has a texture and detail that can't be matched by foam. Natural materials (dirt, sand, and rocks), poly fiber, grass mats, grass tufts, and other materials can all be blended and combined for various effects.

We'll look at several methods, but space is too limited to explore all the possibilities (see the books listed on page 95 for in-depth details).

Start by getting all essential materials together, **12**. First, you'll need earth-colored flat latex paint. Common household interior paint is perfect for this—it can be the cheapest brand in the paint store. The key is that it should be water-based and flat (don't use gloss, semigloss, or satin paints). The color isn't critical—it can range from dark to medium earth brown to dark or medium tan. This paint can be used full strength, or you can dilute it with water (up to 3 parts paint and 1 part water).

You'll also need several brushes: a few inexpensive 2", 3", and 4" brushes will work just fine, as will foam brushes of various sizes. Again, don't waste money on high-quality brushes.

You have several options for scenery adhesive. This needs to be water-based, thin enough to soak into scenic materials, and must dry clear with a matte or dull sheen. You can use a ready-mixed product such as Woodland Scenics Scenic Cement, or you can make your own by mixing

23 Mist the ballast with 70 percent isopropyl alcohol. Make sure it is saturated.

24 Dribble diluted white glue along the sides and down the middle of the track, again making sure the ballast is thoroughly saturated.

25 This Bachmann Scene Shapes walnut, Walthers Scene Master elm, and Woodland Scenics light green are just several examples of ready-made trees that are available from various companies.

26 To seal natural armatures, dip them in thinned matte medium. Here, James McNab treats an armature from Super Trees. *James McNab*

27 Brooks Stover makes trees starting with twigs (left). Adding stretched poly fiber provides fine branch structure (center). Spraying this with adhesive and sprinkling ground foam provides a finished tree (right). *Brooks Stover*

either white glue or artist's matte medium with water (1 part glue to 1 to 2 parts water). I use the white glue mix, but feel free to substitute your choice.

You'll need an applicator for the glue. You can use an eyedropper or plastic pipette, but constantly refilling one quickly becomes tedious. Old saline-solution bottles (anyone who wears contact lenses will be happy to set aside a few empties for you) work better than any commercial applicator I've found because the tips make it easy to control the application. Be sure to label the bottle so you know exactly what's in it. Pull the nozzle/cap off the bottle and rinse it after every use to keep it from becoming plugged with glue.

A spray bottle works for some glue applications, but never use them near structures, roads, or other details as the sprayed glue could land on them.

Trigger-type sprayers work best for glue mixes, but you'll still need to clean the nozzle frequently to keep it from getting gummed up.

Another necessity is a wetting agent to ensure that the glue penetrates the scenery materials. If you try to apply the thinned glue directly to scenery, it will bead up on the surface and disturb the materials. Water itself has a high surface tension and will also bead up without penetrating.

The traditional method is to use "wet water," which is simply water with common dishwashing detergent (such as Dawn or Ivory) added to cut the surface tension of the water. Four or five drops of detergent per pint of water is usually sufficient. However, I prefer using common rubbing alcohol (70 percent isopropyl), as it soaks readily into ground foam and other materials, doesn't foam up like soap and water, and seems less prone to

disturbing scenery materials than wet water.

For applying ground foam to broad areas, such as a rural hillside, the wetting agent can be sprayed. Find a sprayer that produces the finest mist possible. I use a small pump-type spray bottle (an old hair-spray bottle), as many larger trigger-style bottles produce larger droplets instead of a fine mist. A wetting agent can also be directly applied with a pipette or saline bottle. This is best if there are neighboring structures or details that you don't want to get wet.

Now you are ready for applying your texture materials, **13**. Ground foam can be applied to broad areas with a shaker bottle (available from Scenic Express, Woodland Scenics, and others). You can also use a jar with several holes punched in the lid. For tight areas, use a small spoon or plastic cup to sprinkle the ground foam in place.

The finished trees look great on Brooks' S scale layout. Note the ground foam around several of the tree clumps. *Brooks Stover*

Basic ground cover

Start with an area where you want to apply a basic scenic texture. If in doubt, get a basic cover of ground foam on everything. The beauty of these scenery methods is that you can simply apply additional materials at any time over the initial ground cover—for example, if you later decide to turn an area into a farm field.

The first step is to paint the bare scenery form (foam, plaster, or Sculptamold) with earth-colored latex paint, **14**. There are two schools of thought on this, and you can choose either one. The traditional method is to paint a small area (a square foot or so) and then sprinkle scenery materials directly onto the wet paint. The paint serves as an adhesive to hold the texture in place. A disadvantage to this method is that some of the material will soak up some paint and color.

The alternative is to paint all the exposed areas, let the paint dry, and then brush thinned scenery glue on small areas as you apply the texturing. I've started using this method, as it seems to use less material.

Sprinkle fine ground foam onto the wet paint or glue, starting with fine texture, **15**. You can create varied effects by starting with soil colors and then progressing to green grass or a green blend, leaving some soil areas exposed. Continue the process by brushing glue in place and adding foam until you have an area completed.

If you're trying to capture an even or closely cropped area, stop; otherwise, add medium ground foam and then coarse ground foam over the area until you get the effect you're looking for, **16**.

Secure the foam by soaking a small area with wetting agent, applied with a spray bottle or pipette, **17**. Follow this by dribbling glue over it, **18**. Repeat this process until the area is saturated. You can add additional light dustings of ground foam over the wet surface.

You can take landscape texture to the next level by applying static grass. This consists of small fibers that represent actual blades of grass and weeds. It's available in many colors and fiber lengths to represent everything from a well-trimmed lawn to long field grass. Static grass works well when applied over a surface of fine ground foam while the glue is still wet.

You can use varied colors and lengths of static grass to create a weedy ditch, farm field, lawn, and many other types of surfaces. Several companies offer static grass applicators, such as the Noch Gras Master, Grass Tech USA's GrassTech II, and Heki Flockstar. These all are battery operated and require a wire placed from the tool to the wet scenery to create a static charge, **19**. They work well, but can be a pricey investment for a small layout.

A good way to get started with static grass is Noch's simple squeeze bottles that give fibers a static charge, **20**. Load the bottle with static grass, hold

29

This realistic river scene on *Model Railroader*'s HO Turtle Creek project layout grabs a lot of attention. *Bill Zuback*

it about 3" above the still-wet ground foam, and squeeze the bottle to "poof" the static grass onto the surface. Repeat the process, moving the applicator along the surface. With the initial layer of ground foam, it doesn't take much static grass to create a realistic appearance (see photo on page 63).

Natural materials

Many types, colors, and textures of rocks, sand, gravel, and talus are available from Woodland Scenics, Arizona Rock & Mineral, and others. I've become a big fan of tube sand, which is available from home improvement stores. This fine, graded, dried sand can be used for forming riverbeds and banks, as well as for making a base for other scenery areas such as dirt roads and parking lots. It's also inexpensive: you can get a 50 to 70 pound bag for under $10.

A stroll into your backyard, along a gravel road, in a farm field, or into the woods can provide you with dirt and

gravel of many colors. You'll be able to use it for making farm fields, dirt roads, parking lots, riverbeds, and lakebeds.

To ensure that it's dry—and to kill any critters (or their eggs) lurking in it—it's a good idea to bake it in an oven. Spread the material on an old baking sheet, set the oven to 250 degrees, and leave it in there for an hour or two, stirring it occasionally to ensure that it dries properly. Once it cools, you can sift the material through progressively finer wire screen or sieves to sort it by texture. Then separate it by color and texture and store it in old plastic containers.

Ballast

Ballast in many colors and textures is available from Arizona Rock & Mineral, Highball Products, Woodland Scenics, and others. Use fine texture for N and HO and medium for O scale (if in doubt, use the finer texture).

Start by using a small cup or spoon to carefully sprinkle the ballast along

the shoulder of the track and then between the rails, **21**. Use a soft brush to spread the ballast evenly, making sure the shoulder contour looks good and that the roadbed is completely covered, **22**.

Wet the ballast with isopropyl alcohol, using either a misting spray bottle or a pipette. Be careful not to disturb the ballast, **23**. Drip diluted white glue along the ballast shoulders and between the rails, **24**. Make sure the ballast is thoroughly saturated with glue. It will appear white, but it becomes clear and flat when it dries. When the glue dries (give it at least 24 hours), go over the tops of the rails with a track cleaner.

Trees

Ready-made trees in many styles and sizes are available from AMSI, Bachmann, Faller, Grand Central Gems, JTT Miniature Tree, N Scale Architect, Noch, Scenic Express, Timberline, Walthers, Woodland Scenics, and

Plaster makes a nice, smooth bed, and you can fill any gaps or cracks with spackle. Note how the scenery comes down to the riverbed edge. *Bill Zuback*

Paint the riverbed flat black and then glue rocks, twigs, and any other details in place. Make sure the surface is completely sealed. *Bill Zuback*

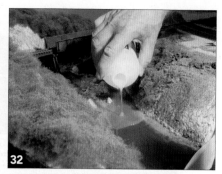

Pour a thin coat of Woodland Scenics Realistic Water in place. Once it dries, add waves by brushing Water Effects over the top. *Bill Zuback*

Paint your backdrop a sky blue color with a roller. Work slowly to make sure the coverage is even and then add a second coat after the first dries.

Trees and foliage work well for hiding the bottom edge of the backdrop. This is James McNab's HO layout. *James McNab*

others, **25**. This is the quickest way to populate your layout with trees, but it's also the most expensive. Making your own trees isn't difficult, and doing so can be quite cost effective.

Tree kits are available from the mentioned manufacturers, or you can make your own trees from a variety of materials. There are dozens of methods for making trees, with the same basic idea: start with a trunk or branch structure (armature), paint it dark gray (if needed), and attach simulated leaf material to the branches.

Commercial armatures are made from plastic, wire, cast-metal, and natural materials. You can find your own natural armatures as well—they are sometimes no farther away than your backyard or a nearby wooded area. Look for shrubs, brush, and fallen branches for the proper shape and size.

When using natural materials, it's a good idea to seal them to keep them

from drying out and disintegrating over time. You can paint them, or if the natural color is what you're looking for, dip each armature in thinned matte medium (2 parts water, 1 part matte medium) for several seconds, and then hang them or set them aside to dry, **26**.

Paint armatures, if necessary, with flat dark gray or grimy black paint (looking at real trees, you'll notice most bark is dark gray, not brown).

To add leaf and fine branch texture, take small pieces of green poly fiber and pull it out, teasing it as when making brush, **27**. Glue pieces between and among the armature's larger branches with matte medium or Scenic Glue.

Spray the poly fiber with Scenic Cement or thinned matte medium (work over old newspapers to catch overspray). Then sprinkle fine ground foam or Scenic Express fine green flocking over the tree. Work over a small container or shoebox to catch

and reuse the flocking that falls off. You can repeat the gluing and flocking steps until the tree has enough texture.

Plant trees by drilling a hole and inserting a pin or piece of wire in the base of the trunk. Then, drill or poke a hole in the scenery base for the pin. Add a bit of white glue to secure it. If needed, glue some ground foam around the tree base to hide any gaps, **28**.

Water

There are many good products and techniques for re-creating water in miniature, which is good because there are many types of water that you may want to model, including streams, ponds, rivers, lakes, and oceanfronts. We can't cover all the methods, but here are a few ideas to get you going in creating realistic-looking water, **29**.

When modeling almost any body of water, make sure the base for it is level (about the only exception is a river

35 You can glue photos onto backdrops—in this case, buildings on either side of the 3-D building. The clouds are also part of a photo turned into a poster print for the backdrop.

going down a rapids). There's no way to make a slanted lake look realistic, and if you're pouring resin to simulate water, the water material will level itself—regardless of how uneven the bed is.

A coat of plaster poured in the bed provides a nice, even base, **30**. Pour the plaster in place and let it level itself. Then use sanding blocks to smooth any undulations after it dries, and fill any gaps or cracks with spackle.

Paint the water surface flat black and let it dry, **31**. For rivers (or lakes near the shore), you can add rocks, talus, branches, and other debris. Glue these items in place with matte medium.

Woodland Scenics Realistic Water is easy to use: simply pour it in place, **32**. A thin coat (no more than ⅛") is all that's needed, although you can add additional layers after the first one has dried. The material will dry smooth, but you can easily add waves by brushing either Woodland Scenics Water Effects or acrylic gloss medium over the surface and then stippling it with a brush.

Backdrops
Chapter 7 discussed adding a backdrop as part of the benchwork. You should always include a backdrop when a layout is on a shelf or along a wall. And use backdrops as view blocks as needed on table-style layouts.

Backdrops don't have to be extremely well detailed to be effective. Even if you do nothing but paint the backdrop a sky blue color, you've given your layout a more realistic appearance than looking at a bare wall. Choose a color that looks like a bright sky blue under the lighting in your layout area. Use flat interior latex—as with scenery, you want to avoid gloss or satin finishes.

A roller is the best way to apply paint to the backdrop, **33**. (You should actually do this step before adding any scenery.) Apply the paint evenly, and add a second coat for the best appearance. Interior latex will adhere to almost any backdrop material, including hardboard, plywood, MDF, foam core, and sheet styrene.

How you proceed after that depends upon the type of scenery you're modeling. You can carry the scenery right up to the backdrop itself. A row of trees or other foliage does a good job of hiding the seam, **34**.

Many modelers print photos of structures, hills, trees, and other scenic details onto matte paper and glue them to the backdrop using a spray adhesive (such as 3M Super 77), **35**.

You can paint hills and other scenic contours on a backdrop. The key is to use colors that match the colors of the abutting ground texture and trees.

Final details
Your model railroad is, of course, not finished by any means. Your layout will improve as you add roads, buildings, vehicles, figures, and other details. You'll find additional ideas for adding scenery in the sources listed below.

More Information
Basic Scenery for Model Railroaders, Second Edition, by Lou Sassi (Kalmbach, 2014)

Building Scenery with Paul Scoles (Carstens/White River Productions, 2014)

Easy Model Railroad Scenery Projects (Kalmbach, 2016)

How to Build Realistic Model Railroad Scenery, Third Edition, by Dave Frary (Kalmbach, 2005)

Mastering Scenery Basics: Backdrops (video), Model Railroader Video Plus (kalmbachhobbystore.com)

Painting Backdrops for Your Model Railroad by Mike Danneman (Kalmbach, 2008)

Planning Scenery for Your Model Railroad by Tony Koester (Kalmbach, 2008)

Model railroading suppliers

Accucraft
accucraft.com

Accurail
accurail.com

A-Line/Proto Power West
ppw-aline.com

Amaco
amaco.com

American Model Builders
laserkit.com

American Models
americanmodels.com

Arizona Rock & Mineral
rrscenery.com

Athearn
athearn.com

Atlas Model Railroad Co.
atlasrr.com

Atlas O
atlaso.com

Bachmann
bachmanntrains.com

Badger Air-Brush Co.
badgerairbrush.com

Blackstone Models
blackstonemodels.com

Blair Line
blairline.com

BLMA Models
blmamodels.com

Bowser
bowser-trains.com

Broadway Limited Imports
broadway-limited.com

B.T.S.
btsrr.com

Caboose Industries
cabooseind.com

City Classics
cityclassics.biz

Classic Metal Works
classicmetalworks.com

Con-Cor
con-cor.com

CVP Products
cvpusa.com

Dallee Electronics
dallee.com

Deluxe Innovations
deluxeinnovations.com

Design Preservation Models
(see Woodland Scenics)

Digitrax
digitrax.com

Durango Press
(see JL Innovative Design)

ESU
esu.eu

ExactRail
exactrail.com

Faller
(see Wm. K. Walthers)

Fox Valley Models
foxvalleymodels.com

GC Laser
gclaser.com

Grass Tech USA
grasstechusa.com

Hartland Locomotive Works
h-l-w.com

Heki
(see Wm. K. Walthers)

Hobby Innovations
hobbyinnovations.com

Homabed
(Cascade Rail Supply)
cascaderailsupply.com

Homasote Corp.
homasote.com

Hornby
hornby.com

Hot Wire Foam Factory
hotwirefoamfactory.com

InterMountain
intermountain-railway.com

JL Innovative Design
jlinnovative.com

Kadee
kadee.com

Kalmbach Publishing Co.
kalmbach.com

Kato U.S.A.
katousa.com

Life-Like
(see Wm. K. Walthers)

Lionel
lionel.com

Loksound
(see ESU)

Märklin
marklin.com

Micro Engineering
microengineering.com

Micro-Mark
micromark.com

Micro-Trains Line
micro-trainsline.com

Midwest Products
midwestproducts.com

Model Rectifier Corp.
modelrectifier.com

Moloco
molocotrains.com

MTH Electric Trains
mthtrains.com

NCE
ncedcc.com

Noch
(see Wm. K. Walthers)

P-B-L
p-b-l.com

Precision Scale Co.
precisionscaleco.com

Rapido Trains
rapidotrains.com

Reboxx
reboxx.com

Red Caboose
(for N, see Fox Valley Models;
for HO, see InterMountain)

Rivarossi
(see Hornby)

River Raisin Models
riverraisinmodels.com

Rix Products
rixproducts.com

Roundhouse
(see Athearn)

S-Helper Service
(see MTH)

San Juan Car Co.
sanjuancarco.com

Scenery Unlimited
sceneryunlimited.net

Scenic Express
scenicexpress.com

Shinohara
(for HO, see Wm. K. Walthers;
for S, see Scenery Unlimited)

Smalltown USA
(see Rix Products)

SoundTraxx
soundtraxx.com

Stewart Hobbies
(see Bowser)

Tangent Scale Models
tangentscalemodels.com

Testor Corp.
testors.com

Tomalco Track
tomalcotrack.net

USA Trains
usatrains.com

Vallejo
acrylicosvallejo.com

Wm. K. Walthers
walthers.com

Woodland Scenics
woodlandscenics.com

Xuron Corp.
xuron.com